REAL PEOPLE
REAL RECOVERY

Overcoming Addiction in Modern America

Eric Spofford & Piers Kaniuka

Prologue by **Dr. Bruce Alexander**

J.ROSS PUBLISHING

Copyright © 2019 by Eric Spofford

ISBN-13: 978-1-60427-166-9

Printed and bound in the U.S.A. Printed on acid-free paper.

10 9 8 7 6 5 4 3 2 1

The Library of Congress Cataloging-in-Publication Data can be found on the WAV section of the publisher's website at www.jrosspub.com/wav.

Phone: (954) 727-9333
Fax: (561) 892-0700
Web: www.jrosspub.com

To all those who lost their lives to the opioid epidemic

—Eric and Piers

CONTENTS

Dedication. iii

Acknowledgments. ix

Prologue xi

Chapter 1: Introduction. 1

How Did We Get Here? 1

Chapter 2: Eric's Story 5

The Escalation 7

Admitting I Had a Problem 8

My Dad's Stroke. 9

Same Old Routine 10

The Methadone Farce 10

A Spark of Hope 11

A New Beginning. 13

Chapter 3 Piers's Story. 15

Moving to Maine 16

College Days. 17

Trying to Kick the Habit. 18

Rebuked. 21

A New Beginning. 22

Chapter 4: Eric and Piers. 25

Being Understood 25

Reconnecting 27

Granite Recovery Centers. 28
Together Again. 29

Chapter 5: The 12 Steps Revisited **31**

Chapter 6: RID and the 12 Steps **41**
Step 1. 44
Step 2. 44
Step 3. 45
Step 4. 45
Step 5. 46
Steps 6 and 7. 47
Steps 8 and 9. 47
Steps 10, 11, and 12. 49

Chapter 7: Spiritual, Not Religious **53**
The Oxford Group. 54
William James and *The Varieties of Religious Experience* 56
Spirituality, Not Religion 59
The Jungian Perspective. 60
Moral Psychology 63
Hardwired for Spiritual Experience 65

Chapter 8: Dates and Trends. 69
Timeline 70
Summary. 75

Chapter 9: The Dislocation Theory of Addiction **79**
Loss of Community. 79
Digital Dangers 80
Stress and Alienation. 81
Understanding Dislocation Theory 82
Individual Selfishness Versus Societal Sin. 90

Chapter 10: Big Pharma. 93
The Medicalization of Human Suffering 94
Pseudoaddiction and Other Tall Tales. 97
Pill Mills 98
Summary. 103

Chapter 11: The War on Drug Addicts 105

Identification 107
Ostracism 107
Confiscation 108
Concentration 110
Annihilation 114

Chapter 12: Perils and Pitfalls 117

Healing the Brain 120
Digital Addiction 122
Recovery and Initiation 125

Chapter 13: What Is Success? 129

Only a Small Percentage Seek or Receive Help 129
Lack of Quality Treatment Facilities 130
Defining Success 131
Innovation and Activism 135
A Call to Arms 137

Chapter 14: How to Choose a Treatment Center 141

The Appropriate Staff 142
Community 143
Family Support 144
Medication-Assisted Treatment (MAT) 145
Access to Treatment 148
Free Services 148
Aftercare 149

Chapter 15: The Mission of the Tribe 151

Recovered—Rather Than Recovering 152
Service—Inside and Outside the Halls 153
Eric Shares His Story 153
The Power of the Recovered Activist 154
A Greater Mission 156

Chapter 16: Real People Real Recovery 159

Calvin's Story 160
Carolyn's Story 162
John's Story 165

James's Story 168
Randy's Story 171
Alex's Story 173
Joe's Story 175
Summary 179

Chapter 17: Conclusion **181**
The Spiritual Question 181
The Power of Dislocation Theory 183
Growing the Tribe 186

Images **187**
Bibliography **203**
Index **205**

ACKNOWLEDGMENTS

This book has been many years in the making. The authors would like to acknowledge some of the many folks who helped make it possible. Not unlike raising a child, recovery *takes a village*—no one heals in isolation. This is especially true of Piers and Eric. They were blessed with great sponsorship and owe a great deal to their respective sponsors, Chris S. and Jerry E. They are also the direct beneficiaries of the tireless work of Don Pritts (1934–2005), one of AA's most trusted and humble servants.

These acknowledgments would run for many pages if we were to thank all of our fellows in AA. We would be nothing without the love, support, and humor that was showered upon us from the very beginning. Recovery is nothing if it does not involve friendship and camaraderie. We have been amply blessed in this respect. Piers would like to give a special shout-out to his oldest comrade in recovery, Mike Breault, and to the men of the Liberation Institute. Their friendship has made it all worthwhile.

We are blessed to be a part of the Granite Recovery Centers team. It would be hard to overstate how strenuous it is to work in recovery in the age of an opioid epidemic. It is one part emergency room, one part psych ward, and one part spiritual retreat. The tragic meets the miraculous on a nearly day-to-day basis. We are enormously proud and humbled by the work our colleagues do every day, 365 days a year.

We would like to extend a special thanks to Dr. Bruce Alexander, whose Dislocation Theory literally gave us a new lease on life. His work has not only answered many of the questions that plagued us, it also afforded us some much-needed direction. Connection is indeed the opposite of addiction. We hope this book will do justice to his theory and bring us into relationships with fellow travelers—both here and abroad.

This book could never have been completed without the help of our trusted editor, Dave Wedge. Dave brought some much-needed professionalism to the enterprise. He has also shown a great deal of patience. We readily confess that we are both supremely opinionated royal pains in the ass. Thank you for your expertise—and for your forbearance.

Eric would like to thank his unwavering and supportive family. They have put up with sharing him with his work more than any family should have to.

Piers would like to give a special thanks to his wife, Jessica. She has always been his fiercest advocate. She has more faith in her husband than he has in himself.

Finally, we want to thank all of the many, many clients that we have had the privilege of working with over the years. You have given our lives meaning and purpose. We love you and will do whatever we can to help you share your recovery with the world at large. It is up to you to lead us out of this crisis. We know you will do it.

Eric Spofford
Piers Kaniuka
March 13, 2019

PROLOGUE: FEELING
A PARADIGM SHIFT

By Dr. Bruce Alexander

For a century at least, popular and professional thinking about addiction has centered on *addictive drugs* and their effects. Heroin, for example, has been said to produce irresistible pleasure in the brain, followed by withdrawal symptoms so painful that finding relief overrode all other human motivations. Heroin policy and treatment was derived from one or another variation on this theme: jail the pushers, drastically restrict medical prescribing of opioids, make the drug addicts suffer through their cravings and withdrawal symptoms, and push them into treatment (if they could afford it) in the faint hope that they might somehow become normal again—or at least manageable.

I am old enough to have followed some of this history first hand. My own introduction to drug addiction came from a Batman comic book in 1950—I was 10. My favorite superhero caught up with villains in downtown Gotham City when they were beating up a "junkie"—a new word for me. Batman hid behind a building while the villains finished what they were doing. Sometime later, Batman and Robin apprehended the villains in the midst of a bank robbery and brought them to justice.

All was well again in Gotham City, but a serious problem lingered in my juvenile understanding. Batman always intervened when villains were harming somebody. Why did he not rescue that junkie? Besides that, what was a junkie?

I asked my father, who explained how drug addicts were so ruined by a drug called heroin that neither Batman nor anybody else cared what happened to them. He explained that drug addicts were villains themselves. They will commit any kind of crime because all they care about is heroin.

I asked my father if he, personally, cared if somebody beat up a junkie. He hesitated, then answered, "No." I still remember that moment vividly, seven decades later. He knew he was shocking me, but he had to tell the truth. He quickly added that in their drugged state, junkies would not really feel pain, so it didn't matter. My father was a compassionate man and a deep thinker, even though, by virtue of being human, he was not always right.

After other cultural lessons about addiction, I eventually arrived at graduate school in psychology early in the 1960s. There, I relearned the same basic Batman story about heroin—except that it was being expressed in the language of scientific psychology. The story was backed up by extensive research on the production and conditioning of withdrawal symptoms in rats and human beings and in the consumption of heroin by caged rats in experiments. Most professional psychologists of the early 1960s seriously believed that heroin was irresistible to all of God's creatures and that heroin addicts had no real motivation apart from their ravenous appetite for heroin.

In elaborating on this doctrine, psychological and medical researchers in the 1960s were drowning out the small number of wiser researchers, clinicians, sociologists, and historians whose deeper insights into addiction could have exposed the flaws in the brutal narcotics policies that prevailed. Many compassionate people, including my father, had been swept into this cruel and futile way of thinking about addiction.

I first met a heroin addict in 1971, when I was 31. I was armed with unimpeachable credentials: a PhD in experimental psychology, postdoctoral research in a medical school, and training in family therapy. But I was still fully convinced of the Batman story of addiction as expressed in its scientific form. My first solo assignment in a methadone clinic was to somehow talk sense into one of these drug-obsessed, subhuman, yet diabolically cunning, junkies.

As I awaited the junkie's arrival, I secretly feared that he would stab me or use his diabolical cunning to separate me from my wallet, but I could not let that show. Instead, I had been instructed—surprisingly—always to be *nonjudgmental*.

To my great surprise, and contrary to my lifetime of cultural and professional education, a real human being walked into the office, announced that he was the heroin addict, and sat down to talk with me.

I did not *unlearn* all my previous lessons about addiction in that first meeting. But after several years of working with heroin-using men and women, I gradually came to think that I had been badly misinformed. Addicted people were fully human and they had many real-life concerns other than their drug use. Moreover, they were eager to tell their life stories truthfully to someone who was actually listening. They felt pain all right, although they frequently endured it with admirable bravery. They were often guilty of stealing, prostitution, neglecting their families, gross selfishness, and deceit—and they suffered deep remorse. But as they often pointed out, none of that entirely separated them from us *straight* citizens. Many had grown up in terrible environments characterized by family dysfunction, child abuse, degrading poverty, and hopelessness.

When I realized that my attempts at treatment were not going to cure any significant number of addicts, I quit psychotherapy. However, I continued associating regularly with heroin-addicted men and women through a local organization that we called *The Concerned Citizens Drug Study and Education Society*. Our little group with the ponderous name was devoted to arguing against the harsh, counterproductive restrictions on obtaining methadone by prescription in Vancouver in the 1970s and 1980s.

Under these conditions, I knew junkies as companions in political activism—rather than as subhumans, clinical patients, or research subjects. Some of my drug-using companions had terrible personal problems, but I became increasingly convinced that Batman, my father, and my psychology professors had been deeply and essentially wrong.

My colleagues and I designed some experiments in our rat laboratory to check out the junkie's stories that seemed to contradict the Batman story. The textbook experiments of the day seemed to support the

Batman story by showing that even lowly laboratory rats—housed in solitary confinement cages—found it impossible to stop using opioid drugs like heroin once they had started.

We showed, however, that rats housed in a relatively normal rodent environment—which we called *Rat Park*—had much less appetite for opioids than rats housed in the usual solitary confinement cages (Alexander et al. 1985; Alexander and Peele 2018).

However, despite our experimental data demonstrating the great importance of a normal social life in resisting drug use, we failed to discredit the Batman story. The public and most addiction professionals simply ignored us and focused their attention on the updated form of the Batman story that was being developed through avant-garde neuroscience research, mostly sponsored by the National Institute of Drug Abuse.

I concluded that we had no hope of discrediting the Batman story, even though I was sure that it was wrong. So, having pushed that line of thought as far as I could go, I wrote a book on addiction (Alexander 1990) and then gave up the study of addiction permanently—or so I thought.

In the mid-1990s, I cultivated my long-standing interest in the history of psychology instead, limiting my university teaching to the history of psychology for a few years. I avidly read classical perspectives on human nature, starting with Plato. I did not seek out classics that concerned addiction, because my historical interests were much broader. However, without meaning to, I kept coming across insights on addiction that were far more illuminating than those I had encountered in the contemporary professional literature (Alexander and Shelton 2014). These insights carried me even further from Batman's take on addiction. Eventually, these insights, together with the Rat Park experience, coalesced into a perspective that is much more complex than the Batman story, which I now call *Dislocation Theory* (Alexander 2008). You will learn more about Dislocation Theory from Eric and Piers in this book.

When I studied Thomas Kuhn's *Structure of Scientific Revolutions* (1970), I understood that nothing short of a full-fledged paradigm shift would enable society to comprehend the problem of addiction and how big a transformation that would entail.

Thomas Kuhn showed that ignoring isolated facts like the Rat Park experiments is an essential part of how scientific and intellectual culture works its magic. It takes much more than a few experiments to change a deeply entrenched idea—*and it should*. Culture is a stabilizing force that keeps us moving in a coordinated way—in spite of the fog of conflicting ideas and facts in which we live.

But paradigms do shift eventually. They shift if a deeply rooted piece of cultural *wisdom*, which has become embedded in scientific theory—like the story that the sun spins around the earth, the story that the earth can absorb unlimited human waste, or the Batman story of addiction—fails to explain reality and also fails to solve critical problems.

That is what has happened. The Batman story, together with the conventional forms of treatment that it generated, and the *war on drugs* have gotten us nowhere at all. The global tide of addiction has continued to rise steadily despite our best treatments, while the drug war has mass-produced pointless human suffering right up to the present (Grillo 2018).

At the same time, however, many researchers have produced data and analyses that seriously contradict the Batman story in one way or another. No one of these discoveries alone can shift the paradigm, but the accumulation of many of them eventually creates tectonic tremors—even in a flawed idea as deeply grounded as the Batman story (Alexander 2008, 2014).

And now, finally, there are many signs of a full-fledged paradigm shift under way, including this book by Eric and Piers.

I am old enough to have actually witnessed a major portion of a paradigm shift in my own country, Canada. I feel honored that my students and I have played a role in the still-continuing shift from our once-brutal War on Drugs to harm reduction, compassionate treatment, and recovery-based institutions in our own city of Vancouver. When this shift began, decades ago, it provoked self-righteous scorn and ridicule.

Today, Vancouver is the role model for all of Canada and the majority of Canadians now speak the language of harm reduction rather than participating in a so-called drug war. Our Canadian paradigm shift is not yet done, but it is well under way.

The paradigm shift has been under way even longer and has proceeded further in some parts of Northern Europe, particularly in the Scandinavian countries, the Netherlands, and Switzerland. In recent years, the paradigm shift has become visible to the general public in Portugal with spectacular, successful reversals of previously violent and futile policies. More national transformations are on the horizon as we continue to rethink our policies on drugs, addiction treatment, and recovery.

I can feel the paradigm shift on a personal level too. I began speaking publicly about addiction issues in the 1980s. In the decades since then, I have changed my tune but little, although the audiences have certainly changed. People *en masse* are now enthusiastically welcoming ideas about addiction that they would have either rejected or regarded only as curiosities when people like me started talking about them. This past year I was welcomed as a speaker in places that I never would have been invited to previously—including a conference hosted by the Ministry of Justice in Thailand and a conference of doctors in the United States. Many other long-time scholar-activists are feeling the shift occur too.

The United States is one of the countries where the paradigm shift is moving relatively slowly. Of course, the Batman story is rarely expressed in the brutal language of the 1950s anymore in the United States since addicts are less vilified than they were in the past. And it is no longer expressed in the obsolete *physiological psychology* and *conditioning theory* of the 1970s.

But it is still embedded in the 21st-century language of high-tech brain scans and neuroscience, human genome research, epigenetics, and specialized medical treatment. The scientific version of the Batman story continues to be publicized by the richly funded National Institute of Drug Addiction, several American professional societies, the American media, and even President Trump (Hoffman and Froemke 2007; Alexander 2014; Editorial Board of the *New York Times* 2018; President Trump 2018). Unfortunately, although the paradigm shift is progressing globally, American authorities—who should know better than to push these counter-productive messages—may be among the last to know.

Alcoholics Anonymous (AA) is one of the most successful treatment concepts for addiction. AA and the many other 12-Step groups that have derived from it all over the world, restore countless individual lives and families.

However, the 12-Step program alone cannot solve the addiction problem. Like every other treatment, most addicted people refuse to ever try it, most of those who do try it do not succeed, and some people who try it feel their problems have been exacerbated rather than diminished. There is room for further evolution there.

I believe that the central feature of AA-type groups is the 12 Steps themselves, which have proven to be a work of psychological genius, including the faith that some form of God or spirituality must be part of the solution to addicted people's terrible suffering. However, the Batman story is also built into the *Big Book* too (AA World Services Inc. 1959). It is perhaps most conspicuous in Dr. William Silkworth's allergy theory of addiction (pp. xxiii–xxx), Bill's Story (Chapter 1), and the Employer's story (Chapter 10).

As the paradigm has shifted in Vancouver, I have found that I can talk much more easily and openly than I could previously with my AA friends. It is not that they have lost their commitment to AA, but they now see that the cause of addiction does not lie as much in their supposed unique vulnerability to an addictive substance—such as alcohol, heroin, or cocaine—as it does in their dislocation from society and personal alienation. We also talk more easily because I have finally stopped imagining that scientific thinking somehow negates the wisdom of centuries that is crystallized in AA and other spiritual traditions.

A recent book, *Recovery: Freedom from Our Addictions*, by entertainer Russell Brand (2017) exemplifies the shifting paradigm in the 12-Step context very well. Brand, in his blunt and flamboyant writing style, details how he practices the steps every day, prays, maintains close ties with both his mentors and mentees, and has stayed sober for 14 years. He expresses deep faith that the program will work for those who truly embrace it. No trace of the Batman story expressed in the original AA doctrine remains, as Brand interprets it. He understands addiction as a way that he and other people have tried to cope with the bewilderment and disconnection that is mass produced by modern culture. Brand believes in God and prayer, but he attributes most of his newfound strength to control his addiction to the AA steps and fellowship, to his family and friends, and to daily meditation and prayer.

I think that Eric and Piers push the envelope further still. They blend the wisdom of 12-Step practice with yoga and Dislocation Theory in a fresh way that offers new insight into recovery for both addicted individuals and a fragmented society. They identify what I call dislocation with what the *Big Book* calls RID (restless, irritable, and discontent). This identification brings the steps into their proper social context: that alcoholism and addiction are no longer seen merely as a matter of individual *selfishness*.

Eric and Piers show that selfishness is deliberately encouraged and rewarded by the leading institutions of contemporary society. They report that simply teaching Dislocation Theory to addicted people has proven to be a powerful tool because it gives addicts the ideas needed to contextualize their personal experience and to more deeply understand how they came to be addicted. This knowledge can enhance addicted people's relationship to the 12 Steps. They are not merely defective individuals; they come to understand that they are suffering from the same stress and alienation that is plaguing society at large. Eric and Piers are calling for a new movement—informed by Dislocation Theory—that weds the 12 Steps to activism. This seems to me a perfect example of the paradigm shift that I am witnessing here and abroad.

I think you too may feel the seismic energy of a paradigm shift in progress in the pages that follow.

1

INTRODUCTION

HOW DID WE GET HERE?

When you step into a support group meeting, one of the first things you hear is that you should never compare. Just identify.

It's a staple of support group culture: don't try to compare your story to the stories of others. Doing that can lead you to downplay your own situation, make excuses, justify behavior, flee responsibility, etc. It's a classic mistake that many people who are attempting to find recovery make in the early stages of sobriety.

"That guy is fucked. I'm not like him," you tell yourself. Or, "She lost her kids and went to jail. Things aren't that bad with me."

When people do this, they're usually looking for *an easier, softer way*. They're not ready. Whether they admit it or not, they're headed towards relapse. Still, no two addicts' journey to recovery is the same. That's especially true of Eric Spofford and Piers Kaniuka.

In fact, Eric and Piers couldn't really come from more different backgrounds. They're from two different eras—Piers the 1970s and '80s and Eric the 1990s and 2000s. They traveled very different roads on their way to recovery. Of course, there were similarities: both had extensive experience selling drugs, hustling, and playing cat and mouse with the law.

But by the time they met in 2004, their lives couldn't have been more different. Piers was 41 and was working as a program director for a New Hampshire treatment center—with a decade of recovery under his belt.

Eric was a sick, 19-year-old addict on the run from the law and a small army of dope dealers.

But Eric was tired—exhausted, in fact. All his friends were either dead or headed to prison. Eric had overdosed four times that summer. After the fourth one, his parents came to see him in the emergency room at Parkland Medical Center in Derry, NH. His father was angry, but was also sad. The sight of his son broke his heart. His baby boy. The little man he raised to be a tough, hard-working logger like himself.

"What's happening?" Eric's dad, Stephen, muttered through tears.

It was the first time Eric had ever seen his father cry. Eric looked down at his body lying in the hospital bed. His chest bones were protruding. He had never been so skinny in his life. He wondered when he had last eaten. He couldn't recall.

He was 5-feet-11 and weighed a sickly 130 pounds. Heroin, cocaine, and Xanax still coursed through his bloodstream. He was restless. His body ached. His parents' anguish made little impression upon him. All he could think of was how he was going to get out of the hospital. His parents left, hoping their son would sleep off this latest overdose and get back on the road to recovery. Their hopes were misplaced. Eric ripped the IV out of his arm and fled the hospital in his johnnie. He was powerless over his addiction. He went to a trap house and got high.

A few days later, exhausted, he faced the stark reality that he was going to die. He was so tired. Tired of chasing the high, stealing, remembering which lies he told to which people, which dealers he had ripped off and which ones he could still call. It had been several years of nonstop running. At 19, he was dying of drug addiction.

He checked himself into yet another detox center. This one was in Massachusetts. He was in a haze. Cops were looking for him. He spoke to a counselor.

"Where do I go from here?" Eric asked.

It was a question that had a literal meaning in the moment, as in, where—physically—was Eric going to go after leaving detox. But the real question was, "Where is my life going?" Was he going to be another statistic, like so many of his friends who died in run-down apartments in rough, drug-infested neighborhoods in Lawrence, MA, Salem, NH, and Manchester, NH?

The detox counselor called a facility in New Hampshire. Piers answered. After exchanging pleasantries Piers said, "We're going to work you hard. This is going to be the hardest thing you've ever done in your life."

By that time Eric had been *ripping and running* for years. Somehow he managed to feed his addiction, evade the police, and keep his job at his dad's logging company.

"I'm a fucking logger. I'm a hard ass worker," Eric told Piers. "What are we working on? I've been working my whole life."

Eric thought Piers literally meant they were going to be working—laboring. He had no idea of the mental, emotional, and spiritual work that lay ahead. Piers smiled a concerned smile.

"I'll see you when you get here," he said.

They hung up the phone. Piers looked at Eric's intake records that had been faxed from the detox center. He saw Eric's date of birth. "Nineteen," Piers said, shaking his head. He let out a long sigh. "Another kid coming up on the front end."

He knew that with an addict that young, he was not only going to be dealing with the disastrous physical and emotional wreckage of addiction, but also with the naiveté and arrogance of a teenager. The chances that Eric would be mature enough—as a 19-year-old male—to handle the rigors of recovery were low. But he also thought he heard something in Eric's voice. He heard confidence and a toughness in his bragging about being a logger. He felt that he and Eric would soon make a solid connection.

A few days later, Eric found himself sitting in a group facilitated by Piers. He outlined a complex model of addiction that made total sense to Eric. It was, in fact, the first time that anyone had spoken to Eric in a language that he could understand.

"Before that, it wasn't like I didn't want to get better," Eric recalls. "It's that what was being presented to me made no sense. It wasn't going to work."

"Piers had been an addict himself and had gotten better. When he spoke about his addiction, he described my experience. He used like I used, going out to get high one time on a Friday after work and finding himself still using months later—the same kind of things that had happened to me." But it went further. Piers talked about the pain of sobriety. It wasn't enough to just get sober. The only way to get better was to find real recovery.

Eric had been sober before. But he never believed he could find contentment in sobriety. Piers told him that real recovery was possible—if he was willing to work for it. Piers then detailed the path of recovery that had delivered himself and innumerable other men and women from the grip of addiction. That path will be detailed in the pages of this book. It's a program that he has seen work for thousands of addicts.

In this book you'll learn how Piers and Eric got better. You'll also learn how the destruction of *community* set the stage for the opioid epidemic in America. You will come to understand how pharmaceutical companies exploit the hopelessness of addicts to insure a healthy bottom line. You will learn about the role played by the prison-industrial complex and how the criminal justice system effectively disenfranchises, exploits, and enables drug addicts.

But, we will also describe a solution and a way out. A way to beat the game. Knowledge is power—and this is especially true where addiction is concerned.

You will be invited to take your place in a new movement, one that weds recovery and activism.

2

ERIC'S STORY

I was born in Holy Family Hospital in Methuen, MA, on March 1, 1985—the only child of Stephen and Beth Spofford.

Dad ran a logging company and Mom worked part time as an administrative assistant. We lived just north of Boston in Salem, NH, right over the Massachusetts border. I was a pretty happy kid, despite a lot of fighting at home. There was some drinking, although neither of my parents were alcoholic or addicted. But I do remember spending a lot of time in my room at night, listening to them yelling.

From first through fourth grade, I played soccer, but I never scored a goal. In fact, I was terrible. I didn't like sports much and I still don't. Growing up near Boston, everyone is a huge sports fan, always talking about the Patriots or the Celtics or the Bruins or the Red Sox. I really don't care. I appreciate that my friends like it, but watching sports was never, and still isn't, my thing.

I did like to fight though and started at a young age, beating up my cousins at family parties. In kindergarten I got in trouble for hitting a kid—with a Tonka truck.

I was a likable kid, but I was also something of a chameleon. I might be quick to punch a kid, but at the same time I had a certain way with people. It's a talent that would serve me well in my years of active addiction—especially with the cops.

In fifth grade, I got some pretty difficult, albeit not very surprising news. My dad took me out to eat. We were sitting in the restaurant when he told me he was moving out. I remember he left on a Friday; it wasn't long before my mom's boyfriend moved in.

I lived with my mom for a couple years while my dad rented a room at his friend's house. I'd spend the weekends with Dad; I slept on a little bed in the corner of his room. We also had dinner together on Wednesday nights.

Things were kind of rough because I wasn't happy about my parents splitting up. It was around that time that I started selling weed. I was getting ounces and quarter pounds and selling bags to the older kids at North Salem Elementary School, the junior high, and even the high school. I was good at it. But it didn't take long before some kid ratted me out to the school's DARE (Drug Abuse Resistance Education) officer.

My mother tried to ground me, but that didn't work. My dad was pissed and yelled at me, but I didn't listen. I just wanted to make some money and buy cool clothes—JNCO jeans and stuff like that. Things gradually got worse. I fought with my mom a lot. We had several physical altercations and I also fought with her boyfriend.

Eventually, I went to live with my dad—and I lost contact with my mom for several years.

My dad and I stayed at his friend's house in that little room. A little while later my dad bought a small ranch in Salem. It was a humble little place, but it was home and I liked it.

I was partying a lot by then. I was smoking weed and drinking on the weekends. By the time I was 14, I was doing ecstasy at parties. I've always done everything at 110 percent, so when I took ecstasy for my first time, I really liked it and went all in. While other kids were taking a pill or two on Saturday night, I'd take 10 on a Tuesday afternoon.

I got a fake ID and hit the club circuit. Club Boom, a rave spot in New Hampshire, became my refuge. It was a place where I used and sold drugs and made connections with the older kids. I was an old soul and grew up really quickly. Everything took off around that time. I met a lot of customers and suppliers—and I dove headfirst into the rave and drug-dealing culture. I started moving a lot of ecstasy. My life was one giant party that I thought would never end.

One day my friend Matt came over with his girlfriend Kelly. We were drinking and smoking weed. He had a 40 milligram OxyContin pill. We crushed it up and split it, each snorting a line.

I had no idea that with that line my life was about to change forever. I got really fucked up and threw up in the kitchen sink. I woke up the next morning wanting to do it again. The beast inside me had awoken. Opioid addiction was about to take hold.

THE ESCALATION

Six months later, I was using OCs regularly; as much as I could, to be honest. They were hard to get at first, but the more I used, the more other users came into my life—making it easier to find the drugs.

I started getting them from guys in Boston. They were some pretty rough dudes who were robbing pharmacies and ripping off other deal-ers. Some of them were going to the *pill mills* in Florida. They'd fill their prescriptions at the pain management clinics and bring the pills back to New England to dish out to their eagerly awaiting customers. I was always looking to get high and make more money. I was a willing participant in this new and exploding black market.

One day, when I was 15, I couldn't find any pills. All my sources were dry. I got *dope sick* for the first time. It's something that eventually happens to every opiate addict. I didn't know what to do, so I called a girlfriend of mine whose dad was a dope dealer. She was already doing heroin. Her parents were both addicts. Her mother was in recovery but her dad was still an active user and dealer.

I went to her house and she shot me up for my first time. I threw up all over her floor. It was another turning point in my life. Things would never be the same.

The girl who shot me up has since died. She was an amazing musician whose life was cut short by opiate addiction. She wrote a song for me while she was in prison. I talked to her the day before she died in July 2016. She had put together some time in recovery but just couldn't turn the corner.

From the moment I shot up that day, my whole life began to revolve around heroin. All of it. Mentally. Physically. Emotionally. At only 15, I was a full-blown heroin addict.

I dropped out of high school my sophomore year. I just stopped going. I was too fucked up. I hated school and I just wanted to work and sell and do drugs. It didn't take long before I had made a name for myself in Salem, Lawrence, and a handful of other gritty cities and towns along the Massachusetts–New Hampshire border. I was working for my dad's logging company but my real job was dealing and using drugs. It was all-consuming.

I had a lot of run-ins with the cops, but as I said earlier, I have always had a way with people. And the cops liked me, even when I made things hard for them. A detective friend of my dad's had heard some things about me and knew my life was spiraling out of control. He liked me and my dad so he told my dad what was going on. He wanted to try to help me get out of the cycle of insanity before it was too late.

"I want you to know, Steve, that I really like your son. He's a good kid. But he's a heroin addict," the detective told my dad.

My dad asked me about it and I just lied, downplaying my addiction. And I continued to show up for work every day, like a good functioning addict.

By the time I was 17, I had been shooting heroin for two years and was pretty beat down. One day I went to work with my dad in Windham, NH. It was a hot July day, the sun was scorching, and I was dope sick—very dope sick.

ADMITTING I HAD A PROBLEM

I tried my best to hide it and pretend everything was okay, but I just couldn't take it anymore. I was cutting some trees with a chainsaw while my dad was manning the excavator. The heat was beating down on me. My mind raced.

"Dad," I said, sweat pouring off my forehead. "Dad—I'm a heroin addict and I need help."

He looked scared. He stopped the excavator. He knew it already, but hearing it from me made it all real. "Alright Eric. We're gonna get you some help," he said.

I went to an outpatient detox in Bedford, NH. I went through their program twice. It was the beginning of an agonizing cycle of getting clean and relapsing that would ultimately drive me and everyone around me crazy.

That first time, I stayed clean for two months. The day I relapsed, I went to visit a friend named Dominic. I told myself I was only going to his place to say hi. But I knew deep down that I was tempting fate. It's what we addicts often do.

When I got to his house, Dominic was getting high. Of course. I knew he would be.

"How's your stuff right now?" I asked.

"Good," he said, sighing. "Real good."

"Is your guy around right now?" I asked, referring to his dealer.

"Yeah," he said.

"Let's talk to him," I said. "Yo, fuck it. Let's go get some."

I shot five bags of dope after being clean for two months. But I was learning the game—how to lie and cheat to keep playing. Dominic eventually went to prison. He died a few years ago.

MY DAD'S STROKE

My dad and I remained very close, despite my addiction and the havoc I was wreaking in his life. When I was 18, he had a stress-induced stroke. I went to see him in the hospital and he didn't look good. It was hard to see my dad—such a big, strong guy—lying there like that.

When I went over to the bed, he suddenly got pissed and grabbed me by the throat.

"You're fucking killing me!" he said.

I knew it was true, but to hear him say that while lying in a hospital bed made me think; it really got my attention. He had bailed me out of jail and helped me so many times. He put up with so much lying and insane behavior. I put him through hell.

Still, nothing changed. Not because I didn't want it to, but because the addiction was just too powerful.

SAME OLD ROUTINE

I continued using and running around with criminals. I committed my share of robberies and was always a step or two ahead of my rivals and the cops. Still, I caught plenty of cases and was in court on almost a weekly basis in New Hampshire and Massachusetts. I went to jail several times.

My life for the next couple of years became a cycle of stealing, robbing, and hustling to get money to get high—get the drugs, do the drugs, and then repeat. Dad's house was home base, but I also had a trap house in Lawrence where I would crash, get high, package dope for sale, and plan my schemes. I never really sold a lot of drugs, usually just enough to support my habit.

THE METHADONE FARCE

When I was 18, I got on the methadone program at a clinic in Hudson, NH. I was still somehow working for my dad. Every day I had to wake up early, drive to the clinic, and stand in line at a little office building. We were like cattle, all lined up to get our medicine.

Every morning, when I got to the front of the line, they'd call me in and I'd make my way down a hallway to a little window in the wall. They would scan my methadone clinic ID and the methadone would come out of a machine and the nurse would hand it to me. I'd drink it down in front of her and walk out the back door.

Here's the reality: the methadone was just the start of the party. Most mornings, I'd leave the clinic and stop and pick up a 12-pack of beer and start drinking and smoking weed. The methadone itself got me pretty wrecked, mixing it with weed and booze kept me going.

But I always needed to get more messed up, so I would move on to Xanax, Klonopin, or other prescription pills. I spent most nights smoking crack or shooting cocaine. My life had become extremely depressing at this point. I only kept a few people around; mostly, I kept to myself. My friends were mainly just my drug associates. I was really miserable.

Looking back on my time at the methadone clinic, I wonder if it saved me from dying of a heroin overdose. I believe the harm reduction aspect of the clinic probably kept me alive. But it certainly didn't help me get clean.

I wound up picking up more cases. The local cops routinely staked out the clinic looking for people with warrants or wanted for questioning in connection with unsolved crimes. The clinic served 800 drug addicts every morning, so there was bound to be someone there for the cops to pick up or question. It was like shooting fish in a barrel for them.

I ended up getting arrested four times in a month and a half. I went to jail for about a month. Jail was hell because I'd get extremely dope sick. They didn't offer any comfort meds and I certainly wasn't allowed to take my methadone. Every time I got out, I went straight to my dealer, bought a bag of dope, and shot up.

Over the next two months, I overdosed four times. I lost the will to live. I didn't want to go on the way that I was, but no matter how hard I tried to do better, I always failed. I was an embarrassment and a disappointment to myself and my family and friends. I was alone.

A SPARK OF HOPE

After the fourth overdose, I woke up as usual at Parkland Medical Center in Derry, NH. My mom and dad were there and they tried to stage an intervention. But I ran out of the hospital and went on a run (don't think we need to explain this) for a few days. It wasn't long before I was back in detox, at a facility in Worcester, MA. That's when I had my first contact with Piers Kaniuka, the man who would help change my life.

Piers was the first person I had met in recovery who made sense to me. He introduced me to the *Big Book* and step work and taught me the difference between sobriety and recovery. But those messages didn't really resonate with me right away, thus I continued to struggle.

After I finished treatment at a New Hampshire residential facility, I moved into a sober living house in Portland, ME, and was clean for about six months. But before long, sobriety wasn't enough. I was restless, irritable, and discontent. I wasn't in recovery any more—I was hanging on for dear life.

I started selling small amounts of prescription pills while I was living in the sober house. I would buy other people's prescriptions, take what I wanted, and resell the rest to support my habit. I was taking a lot of Xanax and soon started shooting prescription morphine before I finally got back on the dope.

Once I started shooting heroin, I ratted myself out to the guys running the sober house and moved out. I didn't like sneaking around and pretending I was sober. When I'm on a run, I am all in. So back to the streets I went.

I spent the next two years in Portland, trapped in a cycle of crime and addiction. In late 2006, I was on an epic run. I had robbed some dealers for a large cache of OxyContin, Xanax, Percocet, and Klonopin and was in a wild blackout run for about a week. I was living in a run-down trap house with a girlfriend who was my partner in crime—literally and figuratively. She died a couple months later.

One day, around 5:00 in the morning, the cops were called to the apartment and I was arrested in the hallway for weapons possession. At that time, it was normal for me to carry around a butcher's knife in my waistband. I was in a full-on drug-induced psychosis.

I was sent to Cumberland County jail and spent a couple weeks there. When I got out, I went back to the same apartment only to learn that some rival drug dealers had kidnapped my dog and stole everything I owned. My dog, Muggsy, had a really bad cataract in one eye that made him look blind. I called him *The One-Eyed Gangster*.

A few days later, again in a blackout, I met a guy who wanted to buy some dope. I told him I had some and to follow me behind a building next door to my house. I pulled my knife on him and robbed him. He had told me he had just cashed his paycheck so I expected to get a few hundred bucks. But all he had on him was $82. I put a butcher's knife to his throat—for $82.

I took that money and bought a couple bags of dope. By the time I got back to my apartment building, it was crawling with cops. I managed to sneak into my apartment and get high. I remember peeking out from behind the blinds and hiding out from the cops. That was the last time I ever got high. The date was December 6, 2006.

A NEW BEGINNING

I left Maine at 6:30 the next morning. I didn't return for a year and a half. I went to my mother's house in Nashua and detoxed on her couch. I started going to meetings again and met a guy who gave me a job at a call center making solicitation calls for the New Hampshire Police Association. There I was, on the run for armed robbery and all sorts of court defaults—and I'm collecting money for the police.

I decided to call Piers and we reconnected. What was missing in my life was surrender. As soon as I surrendered and accepted that my entire life needed to change—and that my problems were way deeper than just doing drugs—good things started to happen.

I moved into a $600-a-month apartment in a sketchy neighborhood in Nashua. The guy who rented me the apartment let me move in without paying the deposit. I was totally honest about my situation and he was kind enough to give me a chance. I will always be thankful to him for helping me get back on my feet.

I started working the 12 Steps with a sponsor named Liam, and later with Piers, and was soon on my way to recovery. I knew this was my last chance and that if I didn't make real, drastic changes, I would die an addict's death. I knew that untreated, my addiction was a death sentence.

I went back to work with my father and we gradually rebuilt our relationship. Over time, my dad began to trust me and through my actions, we became best friends again. So much so that he was willing to help me to open my own business. In 2008 he helped me secure a loan to buy a three-family apartment house in Derry, NH. It was my first sober living home, the beginning of what would eventually become Granite Recovery Centers.

I figured it would be a safe place where a few guys in recovery could live and get back on their feet. I lived there myself for the first year and a half—working with Piers, building the model for recovery that I've been developing ever since. In the years since, fentanyl showed up on the scene and I've lost too many friends to count as a result. And now, my entire life is about recovery and helping others find it.

In September 2009, I attended a national addiction conference on Cape Cod and was inspired to take things to the next level. It was only then that I realized that I wanted to spend my life helping addicts recover.

Very early in my journey, I came to understand that my problem was never really drugs—it was sobriety. I hated sobriety so much that I would invariably and inevitably go back to getting high.

As of this writing, I've been in recovery for 12 years. In these pages you'll learn how I beat the game and how you can too. It wasn't easy for me and it won't be easy for anyone else. But it is possible. You can be recovered.

It's essential to understand the problem, the obstacles every addict faces, how the system is rigged for failure, and most important, how to overcome these challenges and find meaning and purpose in life.

Once I found real recovery, my life was transformed beyond my wildest dreams. If it can happen for me, it can happen for you or someone you love as well.

3

PIERS'S STORY

I was born in 1963 in Washington, D.C.—the only child of journalist parents. My dad, Russell, was a first generation Ukrainian-American and a World War II veteran who grew up in Philadelphia. He went to Penn State where he received a bachelor's degree in agriculture and then a master's in journalism from Iowa State. He edited the Department of Agriculture's magazine, *Agricultural Research*, for most of his career.

My mother, Mary Jane, was born and raised in Belmont, MA. She earned an interdisciplinary doctorate from Ohio State University and taught high school and college before working as a freelance journalist for the Waterville Sentinel in Waterville, ME.

I grew up in southeast Washington, D.C. during the politically charged 1960s and '70s. We lived in an economically and racially mixed neighborhood. My grade school was predominantly black—I didn't even have a white teacher until I was in seventh grade.

The day Martin Luther King Jr. was assassinated, I remember my dad pushing me onto the floor of the car as we drove through the riot-torn city. Growing up in the midst of the civil rights and anti-war movements helped to shape me as a person. To this day, I am very interested in questions of class, race, and war.

Besides being a nexus of wealth disparity, racial tension, and violence (Washington, D.C. would become the murder capital of the United States in the '80s), there was also a lot of drug abuse in the neighborhood where I grew up. Like many addicts, I wasn't the happiest kid. I experienced my share of trauma and was pretty fearful most of the time. Smoking pot afforded a huge measure of relief from the anguish that was my daily companion throughout most of my childhood. By the time I was 11, I was getting stoned as often as I could. I loved it. It really grabbed me.

Our neighborhood was quickly becoming gentrified, which only exacerbated the anger and frustration of the community. Things were a mess next door. There was a lot of violence and substance abuse; the cops were always being called, sometimes by my parents. I remember the aftermath of a stabbing and witnessed some gun play. Things were tense in my home as well. My parents were constantly screaming and fighting.

MOVING TO MAINE

In 1976 we moved to Farmington, ME. The move was motivated, in part, by my parents' desire to get me out of the city before I entered adolescence. We had vacationed every summer in the coastal towns of Camden, Rockland, and Deer Isle, so moving to Maine made sense since it was safer, slower, and familiar. Needless to say, moving from D.C. to Maine was a bit of a culture shock. Still, it didn't take me long to make friends with the *bad kids* in town.

Although Maine lacked the cultural sophistication of Washington, D.C., I found it to be tremendously liberating. I didn't have to be afraid. I could move around safely. In D.C., I could only go a few blocks in any direction from my house before I had to be cautious.

My taste in music went from Bootsy Collins and Parliament to Lynyrd Skynyrd and Aerosmith. It was fascinating—I had never been around poor rural white people. Most white folks in D.C. were upper middle class. At the time I didn't know the difference between a hippie and a long-haired redneck who smoked pot. I only gradually figured that out.

I am not athletic but I started lifting weights and even played football at Mt. Blue High School. However, my love for the game did little to slow my drug use. By the time I was a freshman, I was a daily pot smoker and I drank to get drunk every weekend. By age 15, I was doing cocaine, PCP, and LSD. I usually partied with the older kids—they seemed to get a kick out of the city boy.

I did okay in school. History and English were my best subjects. I was senior class president and played center on the football team. We even won the state championship my senior year. I was popular and had a pretty girlfriend; I read a lot and worked a couple of jobs. But I wasn't okay unless I was able to get high or drunk on a daily basis. By the time I graduated high school in 1981, I was already a *functional* drug addict.

COLLEGE DAYS

I was accepted at Ohio Wesleyan University and headed off to Delaware, OH. It was there that I really lost my mind in epic fashion. My drug use escalated dramatically. I was binge drinking every weekend, doing copious amounts of LSD, and snorting a lot of cocaine.

My grades suffered and I flunked half of my classes. There was some violence too. One night I was in the wrong frat house—drunk and tripping—and I got into a fight with the captain of the lacrosse team. He threw me out of a second story window, knocked me out, and broke my collarbone. I'm lucky I wasn't killed. In the fall of 1983, I transferred to Evergreen State College in Olympia, WA.

Evergreen was a real hippie haven; I got deeper and deeper into drugs. I started freebasing cocaine and was continually dropping in and out of school. I held some manual labor jobs—working on a Christmas tree farm and as a roofer. But mostly I was dead broke and mooching off my girlfriend. I always found the ways and means of getting high though. I spent my days in the cafés and at the gym, my nights in the bars and taverns.

I lived in the state of Washington for ten and a half years. Sometimes, when things got bad, I'd move back home to clean up for a spell at my parents' house. I'd eat their food, lift weights in the basement, and get a job waiting tables. Then, after a few months, I'd go back out west and do it all over again. In 1989, I finally graduated with a BA in liberal arts.

By then I had made a great weed connection and was selling pot full time. I made enough money to pay off my debts and college loans. I even started taking graduate courses in philosophy and comparative religion. But all along, my drinking and drugging continued to escalate.

In the early 1990s, Olympia was the epicenter of the grunge move-ment. I worked at The Smithfield Café, a well-known gathering spot for the local hipsters. Dubbed the *Fuck You Café*, it was a fairly notorious counterculture venue. We all wore Chuck Ts, thrift store cardigans, and 501 jeans.

It was during this time that I started shooting heroin. I thought I was cool, but I was really something of a cliché. I had been doing crystal meth but was beginning to have a hard time sleeping. So I moved in the other direction and started doing heroin. Before long I was shooting dope around the clock.

Still, I managed to get into the Comparative Religion MA program at the University of Washington. Somehow, I managed to finish my first year of grad school with a full-blown heroin habit. But things got a lot worse the following summer. It was 1994; O. J. and Kurt Cobain domi-nated the news. I was horribly strung out and contracted hepatitis. I was waiting for a $14,000 financial aid check meant to cover living expenses. I knew that if I got that money, I probably wasn't going to make it.

TRYING TO KICK THE HABIT

I decided to kick. I enlisted an old girlfriend to babysit me through the ordeal. I loaded up on Xanax and vodka and went to Oregon to hunker down in a motel (my strategy was to black out for the duration). I warned her that it wasn't going to be pretty—and believe me, it wasn't. For three days I was hallucinating, vomiting, and shitting myself. In a moment of clarity I saw the horror on her face and told her to take a break and leave me to my own devices. She took me up on the offer, saying she'd be back in a couple of hours.

After she left I got on the phone and called another ex, who then called my father. She told my dad that I was in dire straits. My father called me at the motel and talked me into coming back east. I agreed, but went on a terrible bender for a few days before my flight. I got high right up to the moment I got onto the plane. By the time I got to New York, I was virtu-ally walking dead.

I spent a couple days in New York with my ex and her family but soon wore out my welcome. They put me on a plane and sent me to Maine. My mother collapsed in my father's arms at the sight of me. I was gaunt, yellow, and 40 pounds underweight.

The next day I was admitted to St. Mary's Hospital in Lewiston, ME where I would spend the next 27 days. I weighed 149 pounds upon admission and 153 when I got out. I just couldn't keep anything down.

After treatment, I moved in with my parents. For eight months, I faithfully attended Alcoholics Anonymous (AA) and Narcotics Anonymous (NA), went to counseling, and completed a 10-week aftercare program. I gained 75 pounds, got a job, and obtained a driver's license. I was really trying to follow the advice offered by my counselor, my erstwhile sponsor, and the folks I had met at the meetings.

But in truth, I was losing my mind. I was short-tempered with my parents. I was still lying and stealing. Drugs were no longer part of my life, but I was a lunatic. That's the dark secret of sobriety—it is not a solution. Sobriety is not recovery. I had thought recovery would follow from being *clean*. It doesn't. You'll learn all about that in this book.

Things changed after a friend told me about some guy I should meet. "He has what you want," she told me.

That was a line from the *Big Book of Alcoholics Anonymous*. The book suggests the reader should take up the program "if you want what we have." But the truth was, I didn't want what they had. In fact, it looked like I already had it and it sucked. So I couldn't really hear anything anyone had to say; I was especially sick of AA mottos and slogans. I really doubted this guy would have anything I hadn't already heard ad infinitum.

The guy was named Don Pritts. And although I was skeptical, I traveled to Mt. Kisco, NY in May 1995 to attend one of his workshops.

I was impressed from the start. Don was different from anyone I had ever met in AA. He was a plainspoken older guy in his early sixties. He had these runny old blue tattoos and was missing a finger. He was pot-bellied and looked like he might put Vitalis in his hair—a very old-school type of guy.

But he had this amazing presence. He was quiet and calm and very kind. He spoke slowly and deliberately, which was very different from the speakers I had heard in AA. His words landed differently—they really touched you. And when he started taking us through the *Big Book*, it was pure magic. From Friday to Sunday we journeyed through the first three steps.

That weekend I had my first spiritual experience in the steps. After saying the third-step prayer, I stood up and was greeted by *silence*. Prior to that moment, my head felt as though everyone I had ever spoken to was trying to get a word in edgewise. Drunk or sober, my head had been pure chaos. But with the third-step prayer something clicked. I don't know what it was but I am sure that I didn't make it happen. All at once I could see the difference between recovery and sobriety. From the vantage point of the third step, I saw that the racket in my head—the anxiety and stress—was part and parcel of my alcoholism. I had been sober but I was far from well.

Prior to that moment my sobriety had been determined by what clinicians call *affect regulation*. In the absence of drugs and alcohol, I tried to regulate my emotions with food and weightlifting and cigarettes. But none of it brought much in the way of relief. Nothing came remotely close to heroin or vodka or weed. Much to my amazement, relief had arrived in the form of a prayer. I had finally begun to heal.

The *Big Book* says that alcoholism is rooted in *selfishness*. This means that addicts and alcoholics put their feelings and desires ahead of everything and everyone else. It is a tough pill to swallow. It is much easier to play the blame game than to assume responsibility for our actions. Over the course of the first two steps I began to see how my addiction had harmed my loved ones. It was a shock. In the span of a few hours I saw many of the myriad ways I had taken advantage of my friends and family, how I was ruled by my feelings, and how I showed almost no concern for the welfare of others. No wonder I was miserable after I got sober; I was full of shame and guilt—I was *restless, irritable, and discontent.*

That weekend I learned that recovery is not about getting sober. I had been a drug addict for a long time. When I got clean, I was in a world of hurt. I had no tools to deal with the aftermath of active addiction—the frustration, anger, and heartbreak. Now I understood that recovery was about learning to deal with the demons that had driven me to drink and do drugs in the first place.

At the end of the retreat I thanked Don and said, "I can't wait to get back to Maine and share this with the fellas." A group of guys sitting next to Don erupted in laughter. "What's so funny?" I asked.

They laughed even harder. "Nothing, you just go to Maine and tell the fellas," one of them replied.

They knew the reaction my message was bound to provoke.

REBUKED

When I went back to Maine and related my experience in a local meeting, I was greeted with outright hostility. They weren't interested in hearing about restlessness, irritability, and discontent or the difference between sobriety and recovery.

The guys in New York had laughed at my naiveté. They knew that if I carried a strong *Big Book* message into a conventional *meeting-maker* AA meeting, I would piss everyone off.

Some of the angriest folks had 10+ years of sobriety. Prior to that night I had been the new guy sulking in the corner and now, all out of nowhere, I was spitting fire and brimstone!

"You're still new. You need to listen and take it slow," one guy told me.

But their reaction didn't slow me down at all. I ploughed through the steps and was awed by what I experienced. In May 1996, I went back to Seattle and made some ninth-step amends. I met with 14 people in 10 days. I visited friends, former employers, and even a couple of guys I had threatened. I met with three generations of women in one day. The first was my ex, the woman who tried to help me kick in the motel room. Next was her mother. I had wreaked havoc in her life, torturing her daughter and dealing weed with her son. Last, I went to the grave of her grandmother. She was an amazing woman; we were really close despite my addiction. When she was dying, her granddaughter had called me multiple times to tell me that the time was short and that I should come soon to say goodbye. I never made it; I was too busy getting high.

Visiting her grave was one of the most powerful experiences I have had in the steps. Her presence was palpable. I left the cemetery knowing that if I continued along this path, I would never treat anyone like that again. Not long after that, I had the realization that I had *recovered*—that I was no longer being mugged by the thought of using. I have not had the mental obsession since the fall of 1996.

A NEW BEGINNING

My life took off after I finished making amends. I had become very interested in 12-Step spirituality and how to best serve addicts. I got a master's degree in Theological Studies in 1997 and another in Counseling Psychology in 2002. In those early years, I went to a lot of *Big Book* meetings and volunteered at the detox center where I had gotten clean. Eventually, I went to work in the human services field, first with autistic people and then as a crisis worker in the emergency room. Those jobs showed me how the mental health system was basically an extension of Big Pharma. The system was not interested in social welfare; it was in the business of medicalizing human suffering. That really bothered me. It still does.

It was at this time that I met my wife, Jessica. Jessica is what we addicts called *a normie*. Her long-standing interests in spirituality, biodynamic agriculture, and holistic health have enriched my life and deepened my understanding of recovery. It was Jessica who turned me on to yoga in 2006.

For the last 20+ years, I have immersed myself in study, yoga, and contemplative practice. Because of my work, I have had the privilege of taking thousands of addicts and alcoholics through the steps. For the last decade I have been studying with Dr. Robert Sardello, co-founder of the School of Spiritual Psychology; it would be hard to overstate the role he has played in my spiritual and professional development.

However, I have become increasingly troubled by what I have seen during my time in recovery. The problem has gotten worse every single year that I have been clean. Just when I thought things couldn't get any worse, fentanyl hit the streets. The treatment industry is highly dysfunctional. What passes for treatment is either ineffectual or downright exploitative; it is more interested in making money than with helping people. Prisons are full of drug abusers, virtually all of whom are poor or working class. And we created millions of addicts through the reckless over-prescription of opioids, benzodiazepines, and stimulants. What makes it even worse is that these issues are almost never addressed by the media or in academia.

In 2014, I helped my father cross the threshold. During the last months of his life, I had to give him morphine several times a day. Handling the drugs did not even phase me. That's what *recovered* looks like.

From 2013–2016, I served as chair of the department of Transpersonal Psychology at Burlington College in Vermont. While I was there I met two important contemporary thinkers: Robert Whitaker and Dr. Edward Tick. Their work informs much of what you find in this book. During that time, I also discovered Dr. Bruce Alexander and his Dislocation Theory of Addiction. Alexander has given us a much-needed theoretical model to study the addiction pandemic. Dislocation Theory informs much of what we do at Granite Recovery Centers.

In May 2016, I reconnected with Eric Spofford. I had known Eric since he was 19 years old and was really impressed with all that he had achieved professionally and in recovery. In May, I joined his team at Granite Recovery Centers. In these pages we share our vision and our experience— what we have learned after toiling many years in the treatment field.

4

ERIC AND PIERS

Eric and Piers first met in 2004. Eric was 19 and Piers was 41.

"I was nearing the end of my rope in New Hampshire," Eric recalls. "All of my friends were dying or going to prison."

Eric had gone from an in-shape teenager who spent his days logging with his dad to a skeletal shell of himself. He looked—and was—very sick, as the years of heroin addiction and repeated overdoses and Narcan shots had taken a harsh toll.

When Eric first arrived at the New Hampshire facility where Piers was working at the time, he met with Piers in a small office. "So, what are we working on? I've been working hard my whole life. I'm a hard worker," Eric asked, clueless to the mission at hand.

"We're working on you," Piers said.

Eric settled in and began taking part in the daily routine of the facility, including group sessions. One day in group, Piers led a talk about the addiction model—the very one that will be laid out in this book. When Piers started talking about step work, it was the first time that Eric had heard anything that made any sense to him throughout his many attempts at getting clean.

BEING UNDERSTOOD

What was it that Eric heard that made sense and made him sit up in his chair and pay close attention? It was that Piers was a guy who had suffered from heroin addiction and had actually gotten better. He spoke about addiction in a way that matched Eric's own experience.

He had used—just like Eric used. He couldn't control it either. Those were the things that Eric could relate to. But he also spoke of his emotional state in sobriety. He spoke about how he felt restless, irritable, and discontent. He assured the young man that there were ways to transform all the anxiety, fear, boredom, and anger. He said that those emotions were the root cause and that they had nothing to do with the substances themselves.

Eric had been sober before but had never enjoyed it. Piers told him there was a way to not only enjoy sobriety, but to appreciate it—it was called *recovery*.

Piers also noticed something in Eric that was different from other 19-year-old addicts. "He didn't meet my negative expectations of an unmanageable 19 year old," Piers remembers. "He bought into this thing sooner rather than later. And when they buy into it, there's a certain energy. They're manageable, they're good clients to have. They're willing to work. They're not complaining about every little thing," Piers said. "And Eric—he's very intelligent. He's very watchful and he observes things without you knowing he's doing it. He kind of surprised me with that."

Eric went through being dope sick at the facility, but still managed to retain some of Piers's message. He fought insomnia—the physical and mental torture of opiate withdrawal. His mind kept torturing him with the idea that just one more bag of dope would let him sleep.

But the physical withdrawal eventually receded, and his strength—both physical and emotional—started to return. His fear of insomnia dissipated and he started rebuilding some self confidence. Piers introduced him to step work.

Eric spent a month there and worked with a few staff members but Piers and his message was the one that resonated and stuck with him.

After Eric left, he went to a sober living facility in Portland, ME. He felt confident but was a bit scared to leave, because he didn't want to lose the recovery momentum he had built. He also didn't want to go back to New Hampshire because he was wanted by the police for some pretty serious criminal charges.

Over the next two years, Eric had bouts of sobriety and even made some amends as part of his step work, but he wasn't ready to fully surrender to recovery. Six months after leaving Piers, he relapsed and was soon back in and out of detox facilities and jail. He thought he had blown it and was never going to find recovery.

"I made a conscious decision that I was riding this bitch until the end," Eric remembers. "It was psychopathic. I literally told people I was going to jail or dying this time."

He went on a six-month suicide mission and crime spree, doing whatever he needed to do to feed the beast within. Much to his chagrin, Eric couldn't get Piers's lessons out of his head. Deep down he knew he could only get better if he fully surrendered to the process. He eventually made his way back to Alcoholics Anonymous (AA) meetings and reconnected with Piers.

RECONNECTING

They started going to meetings together. They talked on the phone constantly and became friends. Piers would take Eric to yoga classes in Concord, NH. Eric went back to working at his dad's logging business.

"I could see the transformation," Piers recalls. "His health came back. His passion for recovery was beginning to trump everything else in his life. That was evident to me."

Piers became Eric's sponsor. They worked the steps together. Eric was so excited about being on the path to recovery and he decided he wanted to make it his life's work. He had a passion for business and was a natural born entrepreneur—skills he used daily when he was on the streets working in the drug trade.

He and his dad dabbled in real estate and Eric decided to seek a loan to buy a multi-family building in Derry, NH so that he could open his own sober house. Eric wanted a place to live for himself where he would be surrounded by other like-minded addicts who were finding recovery—and the Granite Recovery Center (GRC) was born.

Piers discouraged Eric from opening his own sober living facility at first. He believed that Eric was too young and new to the recovery community. Eric was pretty stable working in his father's business and Piers feared that the stress and challenges of the recovery industry would knock Eric off track and derail his recovery. When Piers expressed these concerns to Eric, they had a falling out.

GRANITE RECOVERY CENTERS

Eric cast aside Piers's concerns, and with a loan co-signed by his father, he bought the property. He continued working for his father nights and weekends, doing side jobs to pay the bills. He opened Granite House in 2008 and became the first resident.

Eric hustled to find clients in need of sober living. His model was based upon what he had learned from Piers—it would be rooted in the 12 Steps as outlined in the *Big Book*. Eric would do step work with his residents. It was abstinence-based recovery; residents could not be in medication-assisted treatment. Clients were expected to dig deep into their souls so as to forge a connection to their higher power.

Eric went to conferences and got referrals from other treatment centers. Granite House soon built a good reputation in the industry because Eric was seen as someone committed to the health and wellness of addicts and was driven by his mission to help others.

Piers continued working in New Hampshire but kept tabs from afar on Eric's progress. He wanted the best for his young protégé but feared the often rough-and-tumble side of the recovery industry would beat him down.

In 2013, Piers took a job as chair of the department of Transpersonal Psychology at Burlington College in Burlington, VT. He kept hearing from people in the recovery community about the work Eric was doing. Eric wasn't happy about his falling out with Piers, but remained grateful for his support and guidance during the early days of his recovery. He knew Piers was someone who understood what it took to find real recovery.

He also remembered their long, deep conversations about *the machine* of drug addiction. They talked about how drug addiction was largely manufactured. They discussed the forces that kept people addicted—the prison industrial complex, Big Pharma, poverty, hopelessness, isolation, failed governmental policies, etc.—and how all of these factors gave rise to our current crisis.

They always shared an interest in the big picture surrounding addiction and recovery. These topics were not being discussed in AA meetings or even in the larger recovery community—and they were never mentioned in treatment programs.

"I had huge respect for Piers and his talent," Eric says. "There was some anger but there was loyalty. It's a rare combination. I was angry with him, but had never forgotten what he had done for me."

TOGETHER AGAIN

Eric also kept tabs on Piers's work over the years. In 2014, Eric saw that Piers was giving a talk in Portland about the Dislocation Theory of Addiction (which will be discussed in detail in this book). Eric went to the talk and they reconnected.

"I was happy to see him. It was a pleasant surprise," Piers says.

"I wanted to see him and hear what he had to say," says Eric.

They exchanged business cards and updated their contact information and promised to stay in touch. Eric was seeing good outcomes at Granite Recovery and was opening new centers throughout New Hampshire. He needed someone like Piers.

"If you keep it up, I might just come work for you," Piers joked.

Eric took him at his word. A year or so later, Eric contacted Piers just as he was about to open his largest facility, the 75-acre Green Mountain Treatment Center in Effingham, NH. It was time for Piers to join his team.

Piers and his wife, Jessica, took a trip up to see the campus, tucked into the picturesque Green Mountains of New Hampshire, and he was immediately sold. Eric hired Piers as GRCs' *Director of Spiritual Life*.

"What the fuck else are you going to call him?" Eric jokes. "He's a visionary in this field."

Piers had grown tired of the egotism that ran rampant throughout the rehab industry. And it was so dumbed down—no one was thinking outside the box. Everyone seemed to care more about making the big bucks than helping addicts get better. He wanted to help shape a new—and relevant—recovery culture. That's what attracted him to GRC.

You will learn all about that culture in the coming chapters—a *new* modality that uses Dislocation Theory to inform our understanding and implementation of the 12 Steps. A culture that is broadly inclusive of addicts, their families, and people from every walk of life. It's a culture that is trying to combat the opioid epidemic with something that is both traditional and new.

"It's about providing a meaningful context for their experience even as they are going through the steps," Piers explains. "They're getting something that is really unique."

If Eric had the utmost confidence in Piers, the reverse was also true. Piers knew that Eric was a smart businessman who could stay true to the model while making it work for everyone: the clients, their families, and the staff. Their reunion was a perfect partnership to grow GRC into what it is today: the largest substance abuse treatment provider in New England.

"We both see in each other what the other can't do," Piers explains. "It's okay that I can't do what he does and it's okay that he can't do what I do. Eric understands the machinations of the industry like no one I have ever met. I've learned a lot from him."

"We play off each other's strengths and weaknesses for the common good," Eric adds.

This acceptance of roles and mutual respect is key in an industry that is notorious for egos, divisive politics, counter-productive agendas, and intolerance. It's a very difficult business to manage—and the failure rate on a financial and a personal level is high.

"Too many people get caught up in pissing contests," Piers says. "We both know what it's like to be marginalized by the larger recovery community."

"It's a space where opinions run to extremes," Eric said. "But it's more than business. We're on the forefront in an industry where people have a large emotional investment."

Together, they walk the path of recovery while developing a model that incorporates the insights gleaned from Dislocation Theory. It's a daily battle and the mortality rate continues to rise. Eric and Piers regularly attend funerals for addicts who lost the fight. They mourn friends and comfort the loved ones left behind. It's overwhelming but they soldier on because they know there is a way out.

"The opioid epidemic is my great depression. It is my World War II. It's happening on my watch," Eric says. "This thing almost killed me and it has killed a lot of my friends. That's why I do it. I want to see people get better. I hate seeing so many good people suffer. I don't ever want to hug a crying mom at her son's funeral ever again. I've been through a lot and that's about as bad as it gets. The sobs and screams of a mother at a funeral home, there isn't another sound like it."

5

THE 12 STEPS REVISITED

Although Alcoholics Anonymous (AA) is a well-known institution, people are often surprised to learn that the 12 Steps are not widely practiced. In fact, only a small percentage of AA members actually take up the exercises that lay at the heart of the movement and are the foundation of its success. This has led to a lot of confusion as to what the 12-Step movement is all about. We maintain that AA is not synonymous with the 12 Steps; 12-steppers actually only constitute a small subculture within AA. That being said, 12-steppers have an unparalleled track record in treating addiction. Unfortunately, this is largely unknown or even denied by the media, academia, and the wider public.

12-steppers have been in the minority since about 1940 when AA exploded in size and grew beyond the confines of Akron, OH and New York City, where it all began. AA's birthday is June 10, 1935—the sobriety date of co-founder Robert H. Smith (1879–1950), a.k.a. Dr. Bob. It must be stressed that Smith and co-founder Bill Wilson (1895–1971) never dreamed that large numbers of alcoholics would be able to stay sober through meeting attendance alone. Nowhere in the basic text of the book titled *Alcoholics Anonymous*—affectionately known as the *Big Book*—does it say that one recovers by attending meetings. Instead it instructs alcoholics on how to use the 12 Steps to become *recovered*.

From 1935 through 1939, AA was the unnamed "alcoholic wing" of an evangelical Protestant organization called the Oxford Group. Founded by Frank Buchman (1878–1951), a Lutheran minister and religious visionary, the Oxford Group sought to revitalize the Protestant church through the adoption of a distinctive set of *spiritual exercises*. The exercises were:

surrender, personal inventory, confession, restitution, prayer, listening, and witnessing. Buchman had no interest in working with alcoholics. And he certainly did not foresee his exercises being taken over and transformed by a pair of alcoholics into a wildly successful program of recovery.

AA emerged from relative obscurity after several events brought it into the limelight in 1939. The first was the 1939 publication of the *Big Book*, which introduced their fledgling movement to the wider world. Another was the watershed article penned by Jack Alexander in the *Saturday Evening Post* on March 1, 1941 that reported how a small group of alcoholics were achieving an unprecedented degree of success in finding lasting recovery.

The movement finally made a clean break from the Oxford Group after AA pioneer Clarence Snyder (1902–1984) started bringing some Catholic alcoholics to the Oxford Group meeting in Akron. This was a problem since the Oxford Group was strictly off limits for practicing Catholics. Attendance at Oxford Group meetings could even result in excommunication.

After some priests expressed their dismay that several of their parishioners were going to the Oxford Group, Snyder took matters into his own hands. On May 10, 1940, he created the first official group dedicated exclusively to helping alcoholics. He named it *Alcoholics Anonymous*. Almost overnight, meetings popped up all over the country. What had been confined to Akron and New York City quickly spread to Detroit, Chicago, and beyond. Success, however, had an unfortunate and unintended consequence. Suddenly, there were more meetings than there were recovered alcoholics to lead them; as a result, emphasis on the necessity of a life-changing spiritual experience through the practice of the 12 Steps gave way to a simple reliance upon meeting attendance. It has been that way ever since.

While the 12 Steps are frequently a focal point of meetings, most AA members have never actually practiced them. The 12 Steps of AA are:

1. We admitted we were powerless over alcohol—that our lives had become unmanageable.
2. Came to believe that a Power greater than ourselves could restore us to sanity.
3. Made a decision to turn our will and our lives over to the care of God as we understood Him.
4. Made a searching and fearless moral inventory of ourselves.

5. Admitted to God, to ourselves, and to another human being the exact nature of our wrongs.
6. Were entirely ready to have God remove all these defects of character.
7. Humbly asked Him to remove our shortcomings.
8. Made a list of all persons we had harmed, and became willing to make amends to them all.
9. Made direct amends to such people wherever possible, except when to do so would injure them or others.
10. Continued to take personal inventory and when we were wrong promptly admitted it.
11. Sought through prayer and meditation to improve our conscious contact with God, as we understood Him, praying only for knowledge of His will for us and the power to carry that out.
12. Having had a spiritual awakening as the result of these Steps, we tried to carry this message to alcoholics, and to practice these principles in all our affairs.

In 1950 AA formally adopted the Twelve Traditions. The Twelve Traditions serve as guidelines for maintaining the relationships between groups, members, other organizations, and the global fellowship. The Twelve Traditions are:

1. Our common welfare should come first; personal recovery depends upon AA unity.
2. For our group purpose there is but one ultimate authority—a loving God as He may express Himself in our group conscience. Our leaders are but trusted servants; they do not govern.
3. The only requirement for AA membership is a desire to stop drinking.
4. Each group should be autonomous except in matters affecting other groups or AA as a whole.
5. Each group has but one primary purpose—to carry its message to the alcoholic who still suffers.
6. An AA group ought never endorse, finance, or lend the AA name to any related facility or outside enterprise, lest problems of money, property, and prestige divert us from our primary purpose.

7. Every AA group ought to be fully self-supporting, declining outside contributions.
8. AA should remain forever nonprofessional, but our service centers may employ special workers.
9. AA, as such, ought never be organized; but we may create service boards or committees directly responsible to those they serve.
10. AA has no opinion on outside issues; hence the AA name ought never be drawn into public controversy.
11. Our public relations policy is based on attraction rather than promotion; we need always maintain personal anonymity at the level of press, radio, and films.
12. Anonymity is the spiritual foundation of all our Traditions, ever reminding us to place principles before personalities.

While the Twelve Traditions serve to maintain institutional integrity, they also handcuff us in our efforts to combat the current tsunami of addiction. Especially restricting is the 10th Tradition, which prevents AA members from discussing topics deemed *controversial*. This means that when we are in meetings we must refrain from talking about important issues like Big Pharma or the war on drugs.

We believe that it is imperative that these topics be freely and widely discussed. So while we vow to honor the traditions as individual members of our respective fellowships, we cannot afford to remain anonymous outside of the halls. We have muzzled ourselves for too long. This is a life and death struggle—and the enemy is not heroin. This is not a war on drugs; it is a war on drug addicts. We are fighting a battle that claimed more American lives in each of the last two years (i.e., 58,000 in 2016, 70,000 in 2017) than were lost in the entire Vietnam War. This is a crisis of epic proportions that is not going to end anytime soon—certainly not in our lifetimes. We have to be willing to play the long game; real change is going to take decades, not years.

Our current drug policies are not working. Our politicians, doctors, and media pundits are completely out of tune with what is actually happening on the streets. This is not a problem that can be addressed without the leadership and hard-earned wisdom of the recovery community. That should be obvious. And not only have the best efforts of politicians and the medical establishment foundered, they have actually made the problem much worse! The opioid epidemic is a modern black plague that has decimated a generation. The emperor has no clothes. Drug policy has failed—miserably.

Policy should be shaped by the wisdom and experience of recovered addicts and not by the avarice of Big Pharma, the prison-industrial complex, and the insurance industry. No one can help an addict like a recovered addict. The 12 Steps are an effective and proven method of recovery. There are literally thousands of *recovered drug addicts*. We have an established track record; we have consistently demonstrated that we possess the skills needed to help addicts recover. But the media and medical establishment act as though we do not even exist! Why? Could it be that addicts are worth more sick than well?

Recovered addicts must assume rightful leadership in this battle. Our voices must be heard outside of AA clubhouses and church basements. Anonymity no longer serves us. Our insularity has rendered us ineffectual. We have to stop leaving decisions about what happens to our brothers and sisters to others. The people who make laws and set policy are never from our ranks. Instead, they are legislators, pharmaceutical and insurance industry professionals, lobbyists, and doctors. People who have never walked in our shoes shape our destinies. And here is the real issue—many of these same people profit handsomely off of our suffering. The treatment industry is a $35 billion business, yet those for whom the industry exists—addicts—have no seat at the table. We have never even been invited. This has got to change. And it is up to us to change it.

We are seeding a new grassroots movement. It will be insistent and vocal and deliberate. It's time to harness our gifts and bring our message to the media, college campuses, and the halls of power. We must establish new organizations that are capable of delivering real change. We must rebut the lie that *abstinence kills*. It is not acceptable that the treatment industry has become an extension of Big Pharma and that there is no real platform for those who have lived the experience of addiction and recovery.

Our goal will be to inform the public about what is really going on, even as we continue our 12-Step work. We are not surrendering our AA (or NA, CA, HA) memberships. In fact, we are redoubling our efforts at serving addicts who are languishing in jails and detox facilities. It is a great honor to be a part of a fellowship that saves lives—a fellowship that gives kids back to their parents and parents back to their kids—a fellowship that transforms junkies and alcoholics into productive members of society. But it is time we take the next step; we must educate the public about the realities of addiction.

People need to understand the causes and conditions that brought us to this impasse. AA has spawned more than 200 anonymous fellowships to help people recover from addictions to everything from alcohol and narcotics to gambling and sex. These anonymous fellowships have helped millions upon millions. But their members could be an even more effective force if they educated themselves about the underlying forces that cause and perpetuate addiction. We need to wed knowledge and spirituality. Knowledge + spirituality = power. That is the formula for success.

We need to tell the story of how we got here. This crisis is not due to Americans' insatiable appetite for drugs. The United States is, by far, the most addicted country in the world. But our relationship with drugs and alcohol has less to do with demand than it has to do with economic globalization, institutional corruption, racism, and the criminal justice system. Over the last 25 years we have witnessed the destruction of one community after another all across the country. Stagnant wages, job loss, and drug addiction have laid waste to cities and towns all over America. The opioid epidemic is but a measure of the despair that afflicts us. People are lonely and fearful in ways that we have never seen before. We may be more *connected* through digital technology, but we are also far more isolated and fearful than we have ever been.

Over the years we have researched a wide range of topics including the war on drugs, the Dislocation Theory of Addiction, and Big Pharma. We have come to understand how socioeconomic status impacts addiction and how Big Pharma and digital technology prime the pump for substance abuse. These are all topics that must be thoroughly debated and discussed. There is an important body of research that needs to be disseminated throughout the recovery community and to the population at large.

The *Big Book* and the 12 Steps will remain our foundation of recovery. But the game has changed and we need to reevaluate our overall approach in the age of the opioid epidemic. AA was once dominated by older white men. Today, children abuse prescription drugs, college students are addicted to adderall, and middle-aged women shoot heroin. Our prisons are crammed full of men and women with black and brown skin serving long sentences on drug possession charges. So while the 12 Steps remain an effective treatment modality, the demographic has expanded to include virtually every strata of society. People are dying at scale. We need to step up our game.

To be truly effective, our movement must enlist people from every conceivable background—from professors and CEOs to felons and high school dropouts—black and white, gay and straight, wealthy and poor, liberal and conservative. If we are to succeed, we must form a broad-based coalition. We must educate the public even as we work to help addicts achieve recovery. Those of us who have been blessed with recovery understand that it is incumbent upon us to spread the good news. But we also realize that it is up to us to change the narrative—that we must step forward and take the bully pulpit from those who insist that opiate addiction is a "chronically relapsing condition" and that "abstinence kills."

Fortunately, there is a lot of evidence to suggest that we are witnessing the beginning of a paradigm shift. Prominent thinkers like Bruce Alexander, Carl Hart, and Gabor Mate are challenging the received wisdom that addiction is essentially a biological phenomenon. Unfortunately, the shift is being felt more in Europe (i.e., Portugal and the Netherlands) than in the United States. That being said, we do see the makings of a new activist movement in the United States. Members of the recovery community are finally beginning to advocate for the majority of addicts who cannot access treatment. Parents are increasingly concerned about the prescribing of stimulant medication to children diagnosed with ADHD. People from across the political spectrum are now questioning the wisdom of incarcerating drug addicts. And sadly, there has been an explosion of support groups for those who have lost loved ones to this dreaded epidemic.

The need for a new movement only slowly dawned on us. Step work revealed to us the reality of real recovery—to the fundamental difference between recovery and sobriety. We knew from the get-go that our ability to help others was a function of our spiritual condition, that we could not pass on what we did not have. But we only gradually came to understand that the system itself was a major part of the problem—that it was more concerned with making money and expanding market share than it was with actually helping people.

We spent years trying to connect with people who we thought might want to help us. We met with doctors and psychologists. We taught college courses. We spoke at conferences and testified before congress. We approached the power brokers of the industry. People were polite but their interest was largely feigned. They were not alarmed by what we had to tell them about what we were seeing on the streets and in the detox facilities; nor were they impressed that we had recovered from the very condition that was taking so many lives. We finally concluded that it was time for the recovery community to take matters into its own hands. No one is coming to our rescue. We must challenge the status quo and speak truth to power.

For the last couple of years we have been bringing the message of informed activism to our clients. To say that they find it compelling would be a gross understatement. It is a message that grabs them by the throat. It speaks to their experience on a macro level. We can get their attention because they know we were once addicted ourselves. They identify with us. Like them, we lose all control once we start using and we are miserable when we stop. Any addict will identify with that. But this new message takes it to an entirely different level—it explains the context and etiology of addiction. It is something that they have never heard before; it answers the very questions that have long been nagging them.

It explains what is wrong with our society. It explains that the internal condition of the addict is actually shared by the vast majority of the *civilian* population. American society is itself restless, irritable, and discontent. We are all anxious and depressed to varying degrees. We are all horrified by what is transpiring before our very eyes. The forces that drive people to abuse booze and dope also give rise to compulsive shopping, gambling, and gaming. These are the forces that are shredding the social fabric.

So what are they? Why is it happening? Why are people feeling so distressed and alienated? Why is sobriety so painful? Why do so many of us feel in need of immediate relief? These are the million dollar questions. We believe that Bruce Alexander and his Dislocation Theory of Addiction have the answers. Dislocation Theory explains how we got here in the first place.

But before we can really grasp the implications of Dislocation Theory, we must first outline the model of addiction that we use to work with addicts, the model we have distilled from the *Big Book*:

Recovered ≠ Cured

Mental	Emotional	Physical
Obsession	**RID**	**Compulsion**
A recurrent and persistent idea that is stronger than and does not respond to reason	Restless Irritable Discontent	Inability to stop once you start
Episodic	Chronic	Damage to the midbrain— nucleus accumbens
Only when sober	Primarily when sober	Progressive
	Progressive	Untreatable
	Can be treated through spiritual practice and meaningful connection	

The cardinal symptom of addiction is the compulsion. Addicts and alcoholics lose all control of their consumption once they start. There is a growing consensus that addiction develops as a result of damage to a part of the midbrain called the nucleus accumbens. The nucleus accumbens is part of the brain's *reward circuitry*, and is directly involved with dopamine and serotonin. Dopamine is associated with anticipation and pleasure; serotonin is related to satiety and inhibition.

Abstinence is the only way to check the compulsion. Abstinence alone, however, is insufficient for recovery. Most addicts cannot stay sober because it is simply too painful. Sobriety actually precipitates the other two symptoms—obsession and RID (restless, irritable, and discontent).

The mental obsession, which only occurs when the addict is sober, is a persistent and recurring thought that does not respond to reason. That means that it is irrational and episodic—that it comes and goes for no reason. It does not matter if one is having a good day or a bad day or how much one loves one's family or fears for one's health, the obsession trumps all. Sadly, most addicts and substance abuse professionals wrongly assume that recovering addicts must contend with the obsession for the rest of their lives. This mistaken assumption has led to an almost universal endorsement of cognitive-behavioral therapy as the default modality in the treatment of addiction. Addicts are routinely taught that they must learn to *think through the drink*.

The *Big Book* assumes just the opposite—that the true alcoholic has demonstrated time and again that he cannot mentally control his or her obsession to drink. That being said, many alcoholics can stay *sober*, even though they are periodically harassed by the thought of drinking. These are the *white knucklers*—men and women who maintain sobriety through grit, determination, and meeting attendance. Their constant refrain is, "Don't drink, go to meetings, and ask for help."

However, the great promise of the *Big Book* is that one can be recovered—freed from the mental obsession to drink. This is what is meant by the term "psychic change." It is what the New Testament calls a "metanoia"—a change of mind or conversion. Still, being recovered is not the same as being *cured*. We cannot reverse the damage done to the midbrain. There is no turning an alcoholic into a social drinker—or an addict into a recreational user. The addict or alcoholic can, however, be freed of the obsession to use.

Unfortunately, this fact is rarely acknowledged by the treatment industry or even the recovery community at large. There are a few reasons for this. One is the relatively small percentage of addicts who actually practice the steps. Another is the vested interest of those who would have us believe that addiction (especially opiate addiction) is a *chronically relapsing condition*. You'll hear a lot about these people throughout this book. They are the ones who deny that opiate addicts can ever find lasting recovery, and instead promote the idea that it is a chronic condition that can only be managed. They claim that "abstinence kills." These are the people who deny our very existence. We are writing this book, in part, to let the world know that they are lying to you. There are thousands of recovered opiate addicts, and our numbers are growing.

6

RID AND THE 12 STEPS

To become recovered one must treat the underlying emotional symptom, or *RID* (*restless, irritable, and discontent*). The *Big Book* states that alcoholics are "restless, irritable, and discontented unless they can again experience the sense of ease and comfort that comes at once by taking a few drinks" (*Big Book* pp. xxvii–xxix). All true addicts and alcoholics know that being a *dry drunk* follows hard on the heels of sobriety. This is why sobriety is the prerequisite, and not the goal, of recovery. Abstinence is but a beginning, and not the end.

RID explains why the addict is always moving toward the next drink or drug. Sobriety is simply too painful. We are obsessed with finding relief. This makes us more or less addict oblivious toward the feelings of others. The dry drunks are not acting this way deliberately, nor are they intentionally trying to hurt anyone—they simply cannot help themselves. They have been conditioned to put their own feelings first. This is why they cannot stop using even though they can clearly see the harm that they are causing their spouses and children. It does not matter how much they love their families, or how much their families love them—addiction is more powerful than any bond of human affection.

Sober addicts suffer from RID, in large part, because they lack coping skills. Getting high is actually the *solution* to life's problems—when a relationship ends: get high; lose a job: get high; or get evicted: get high. At the same time, getting loaded is also their primary means of pleasure. Hanging out with friends is about getting high. Celebration is about getting high. Sex is unimaginable without booze or drugs. The clinical world rightly asserts that addiction is rooted in affect regulation, that the addicts are driven to change the way they feel. That is why, in the absence of genuine recovery, sober addicts often succumb to secondary addictions like shopping, sex, gambling, or working out. They will do whatever they think might take the edge off. All the repetitive compulsive behaviors one sees in sober addicts are but vain attempts to fill the void that was once occupied by drugs and alcohol. Unfortunately, nothing works like vodka or heroin.

Daily life is determined by affect regulation. Everything is about feeling better. This is readily apparent in residential treatment settings. Our clients' lives are usually in complete disarray. Not only must they deal with the painful feelings that attend sobriety, they must also contend with the consequences of their addiction. This could be anything from divorce and homelessness to hepatitis C and imminent incarceration. Rather than face their problems head on, they waste valuable time smoking cigarettes, playing cards, or trying to hook up with the other clients. Tell them that they have a life-threatening condition and that their chances of recovery are not good and they just shrug it off and go straight to the card game or smoking area. This speaks to the psychological dimension of addiction. Addicts put their feelings ahead of everything, even recovery itself! It is all about how the addict feels. The *Big Book* calls this *selfishness*.

Selfishness does not so much mean grandiosity as it does self-absorption. Addicts, especially when sober, simply cannot stop thinking about themselves and their discomfort. This means that sobriety is characterized by an almost paralyzing self-consciousness. Getting high affords an effective, albeit temporary, release from this condition. Addicts use drugs in order to *get out of their heads*. Spiritual modalities work because they can affect a comparable freedom without the use of mind-altering substances. And unlike getting high, genuine spirituality is about cultivating authentic connections with others. The quality of one's recovery is ultimately reflected in one's relationships.

Where the *Big Book* understands affect regulation in terms of selfishness, it sees recovery as a path toward God and neighbor at the expense of self. It is a journey from selfishness to selflessness. This means the addict must get out of the stress response. Getting high is intimately related to stress. In active addiction, we are constantly stressed by the need to get more money and to secure more drugs. In sobriety, we are stressed by the absence of drugs, our primary coping mechanism. Recovery is impossible for the addict who never learns how to regulate that stress. Viewed from this perspective, the concept of selfishness makes a lot of sense. If a person is constantly stressed, he or she will be driven to seek relief. And if soothing oneself becomes the central preoccupation of one's life, it will be almost impossible to form meaningful relationships with others.

Getting high, then, affords temporary relief from the tyranny of the stress response; it causes a spike in the production of dopamine—a neurotransmitter associated with euphoria—in our brains. However, these same regions are also stimulated by compassion and prosocial behavior. This means our brains are wired in such a way that we actually experience pleasure when caring for others. Therein lies the power of the 12 Steps. They heal by facilitating and promoting authentic human connection. Human connection feels good.

But before addicts can reconnect with others, they must first confront the ugly truth of their addiction and the harm it has caused their loved ones. This confrontation is essential. It is the *narrow gate* through which recovering addicts must pass. The New Testament word for truth is *aletheia*. Aletheia means truth in the sense of *disclosure*. The steps require that addicts face the truth, and then share what they find with another human being. Bill Wilson writes that the only people who cannot recover are those who are "constitutionally incapable of being honest with themselves" (*Big Book* p. 58)—or in other words, alcoholics who cannot face the truth.

Unfortunately, family members often unwittingly spare us the very truth we need to hear. They are afraid to tell us what they really think and feel. They think that if they say the wrong thing, if they somehow upset us, we will surely relapse. This is why they tiptoe around us or try to shield us from the stressors of daily life—this is but a form of enabling. It is much better to give addicts the hard truth of the pain that they have caused their families. Addicts must come to realize that they are not the injured parties and they are not the victims—furthermore, they were not even present to the spectacle of their own addictions because they were high or more or less checked out. The addicts' families and friends are the ones who lie sleepless, night after night, waiting for the phone to ring, tormented by the anticipation and seeming inevitability of impending bad news.

STEP 1

The first step reads, "We admitted we were powerless over drugs and alcohol—that our lives had become unmanageable" (*Big Book* p. 58). "Powerless over drugs and alcohol" refers to the compulsion and obsession. Addicts lose all control over their using once they start (compulsion); and they are plagued with the thought of using when they get sober (obsession). Unmanageability refers to RID. Addicts are emotionally unmanageable; that is why they abuse drugs and alcohol in the first place.

STEP 2

The second step raises the issue of spiritual power. The *Big Book* reads, "If a mere code of morals or a better philosophy of life were sufficient to overcome alcoholism, many of us would have recovered long ago. But we found that such codes and philosophies could not save us, no matter how much we tried. We could wish to be moral, we could wish to be philosophically comforted, in fact, we could will these things with all our might, but the needed power wasn't there."

This means that recovery is not a matter of knowing the difference between right and wrong, or having a healthy conscience. Addicts know that they should not lie or steal but they do it anyway. They lack the power to live according to their own moral code; they cannot answer the still small voice within. Furthermore, sobriety, by itself, does not confer moral power. Such is the dilemma of dry drunks. They get clean and sober, but lacking the means to regulate their emotions, find themselves engaging in many of their old *using behaviors* (e.g., lying, cheating, and stealing). Thus, lack of moral power is not a function of getting high. It is not the heroin habit that drives them to do bad things. Rather, it is the *spiritual malady* that prevents the addicts from living according to the promptings of their consciences. This is why the *Big Book* says that we need a "power by which we could live" rather than a "power by which we could stay sober."

STEP 3

Now we can approach the third step and the pivotal concept of surrender. In order to truly surrender, addicts must first confront the reality of their condition, the painful truth of how they have harmed others. This is what the AA pioneers called *ego deflation at depth*. Addicts must surrender if they are to receive spiritual power. Truth is the cost of power. Where Steps 1 and 2 are about confronting the truth, the third step is about spiritual receptivity and spiritual power.

The *Big Book* makes clear that before addicts can surrender, they must first agree to stop blaming others for their circumstances. This is not to ignore or dismiss the fact that most addicts have been traumatized or suffered grievous harm. What it means is that the spiritual path demands that addicts take responsibility for their actions. This involves recognizing that one cannot change other people or alter the past. The *Big Book* reads, "Admitting he may be somewhat at fault, we are sure other people are more to blame." This is often as far as addicts usually get. They admit that they stole the money but they blame the owner for tempting them by leaving it on the table. Addicts are quick to shirk responsibility. The *Big Book* makes it clear that this must stop.

The third-step prayer is a gesture of surrender. It is also an acknowledgment of moral failure and powerlessness. It is recognition that the addict cannot fix him or herself nor can he or she heed the promptings of his or her own conscience. Paradoxically, genuine surrender is invariably followed by an influx of spiritual power. A power made manifest in the writing of the fourth step; a power that enables addicts to see even deeper truths about themselves.

STEP 4

In the fourth step, the rubber meets the road. Writing a personal inventory illuminates the *shadow complex* that has been running the show. The shadow is a composite of all the feelings and traits that the addicts have been hiding from themselves and others. It consists of many negative emotions, especially fear, envy, jealousy, and hatred. The fourth step also forces the addicts to confront their insecurities—their sense of not being good enough, of being unlovable, of being a fraud. Jungian psychology would describe the writing included in the fourth step as an *underworld descent*. The addicts must plumb the depths of their souls in order to find the treasures buried within—the truth that will set them free. The journey is perilous—the addicts must confront and battle the monsters of the psyche in order to be healed. This descent demands courage and rigorous honesty. Facing the truth is essential to recovery; one could even argue that addicts do not so much need to seek God as they need to admit truth.

Although the *Big Book* does not use this specific term, the fourth step is essentially about *forgiveness*. In answering how they have been selfish, self-seeking, dishonest, and frightened (the *turnarounds* or *4th column*), the addicts effectively defuse their resentment. This is a most difficult exercise, especially when the addicts are wrestling with the reality of their own victimization. But addicts must keep in mind that the exercise is really asking how they have *used* the resentment subsequent to the actual event. Did the resentment lead them to punish people other than the perpetrators? Did they use it to justify their addiction? Did it make them judgmental of the lesser sufferings of others? An addict's capacity for forgiveness is ultimately a function of his or her willingness and ability to honestly answer these questions.

STEP 5

Rooted in the Christian practice of confession, the fifth step is almost always cathartic. It usually takes several hours, during which time the addicts unburden themselves of a lifetime of anger, fear, and regret. Whether one realizes it or not, we all have a deep intrinsic need to stand naked and vulnerable before another person without fear of judgment or rejection. Needless to say, most people will never have that experience. Twelve-steppers are blessed in this respect. This is one of the big reasons why the steps succeed where so many other modalities fail.

The steps demand self-disclosure. There is a famous line in the *Big Book* that reads, "... we usually find a solitary self-appraisal insufficient"

(*Big Book* p. 72). It is not enough to know the truth about oneself. Our secrets only lose their power when they are shared in confidence. The addict cannot afford to harbor secrets or hide behind his false persona. In active addiction we wear a mask so as to get one over on our families, partners, and employers. We project an image that is at complete variance with what is really going on inside ourselves. This must be addressed in recovery.

We have to let someone know the truth of what we did, of what happened to us, of what we really think, and how we really feel. Self-disclosure occurs throughout the step process. We do it explicitly in Steps 5, 9, and 10. But we also practice it in Step 12. Relating the truth of our struggles in recovery is often what *hooks* newcomers. We should never try to impress them with war stories. All addicts have tales to tell. Instead, we should share the reality of being recovered, how we got there, and what it is like to walk a 12-Step path.

STEPS 6 AND 7

In Steps 4 and 5 the pendulum swings back in the direction of truth— truth at an even deeper level than what was encountered in Steps 1 and 2. Steps 6 and 7 (an hour-long meditation followed by a prayer) bring another measure of power. This comes in the form of *relief.* Many addicts only begin to feel better after they have read the fifth step. In fact, for many addicts this relief is what finally convinces them of the efficacy of step work. It also provides the energy needed to move forward—toward the frightening prospect of making amends.

STEPS 8 AND 9

After we make a list of people we have harmed in Step 8, in the ninth step we attempt to make restitution to those we have harmed. For most addicts this step causes the most trepidation. Many quit at this juncture. The ninth step may be the most awkward, agonizing, and terrifying step, but it is often the most rewarding as well. We never apologize when making amends. Bill Wilson knew that talk was cheap and that alcoholics are notorious for making hollow apologies. Instead, we are instructed to acknowledge the harm we have caused and to inquire as to how we might make it right.

It is important to distinguish *living amends* from *transactional amends.* Many amends involve seeing people from the past (e.g., ex-partners, former employers, old friends). These amends require legwork but can usually be accomplished in a single visit. We call these transactional amends. We make living amends to family, spouse, and our dearest friends—people who have been part of our lives for a long time and will continue being in our lives for the foreseeable future. Needless to say, these are the people who have suffered most from our addiction. Making things right may take a lot longer with these folks since they have suffered much greater harm. These amends usually require change over the long term. The addicts must *walk the walk.* They must first identify the ways they have harmed their loved ones and then refrain from those behaviors. That constitutes a beginning.

In the world of pop psychology, one often hears that one must "first forgive oneself." This notion does not really hold true in the steps. It would be only too convenient that if, after harming you, all I had to do was forgive myself. This does not mean that recovering addicts should forever labor under a burden of shame and guilt. Rather, we believe that addicts can only stand with their head held high after they have done everything within their power to make matters right. Only then will they be able to face themselves in the mirror. We believe that many addicts relapse because they have not addressed the very real issues of shame and guilt—meaning they have not made amends.

The St. Francis prayer reads, "It is better to forgive than to be forgiven." This wisdom is inscribed in the steps. We find forgiveness in Steps 4–7; only afterwards do we make amends. The steps insure that we find forgiveness before we approach those we have harmed. Addicts almost invariably try to apologize to their loved ones immediately upon getting sober. The steps restrain us from doing this; this is but one example of how the *Big Book* serves as a map to help us navigate the interpersonally treacherous waters of early recovery.

There is no guarantee that we will be forgiven by those we visit in Step 9. Making amends is not so much about seeking forgiveness as it is about acknowledgment, restitution, and change. That being said, addicts are frequently forgiven by those they approach. Most people want to forgive; they are just like us—they want to be freed of the burden of resentment.

Everything starts to pivot away from the addict in the ninth step. He has reached a point where he can begin to be of service to others. Having completed the first nine steps, he now has a unique skill set to help those suffering from addiction.

STEPS 10, 11, AND 12

White Bison, a Native American 12-Step movement, asserts that the last three steps are about *change*. Having cleaned the wreckage of the past in Steps 4–9, addicts are ready to return to life and its myriad challenges. They are also ready to assume a measure of responsibility for the still suffering addict. They must continually practice what they have learned thus far if they are going to become an effective sponsor. In the tenth step, addicts refine the inventory skills they learned in Step 4. They learn how to use inventory to help negotiate the challenges of daily life.

Step 11 is about deepening one's relationship with God. While it makes specific reference to prayer and meditation, the eleventh step may include any number of other practices. Many addicts incorporate their religious practice into the eleventh step. Others read spiritual literature on a daily basis. Some addicts make time to commune with nature. Over the last several decades, large numbers of addicts have turned to Eastern disciplines like yoga or tai chi.

We are only beginning to understand the degree to which addiction is related to the stress response. Recovery demands that addicts find a measure of peace and serenity, that they find a way out of the stress response so that they can be genuinely present with others. Those of us who ascribe to the Dislocation Theory of Addiction (which will be discussed at length in upcoming text) believe that many addicts are so stressed and alienated that they find it easier to be alone (with or without drugs) than to interact with others. Recovery takes us in the opposite direction—away from drugs and toward our fellow human beings. This meme is beginning to gain traction in the wider recovery world. Today, one often hears, "The opposite of addiction is not sobriety, but connection." This saying captures something essential about the nature of recovery.

The steps help us forge connection in a number of significant ways. They bring us into relationship with our higher power, with the truth about ourselves, and with others. Steps 5 and 9 go a long way toward freeing us from the tyranny of the stress response. However, the steps do not bring us into a healthy connection with our bodies. Addicts are estranged from their physical selves—they are *head people*. That is largely due to trauma and the stress response. Neuropsychology reveals that prolonged stress and anxiety leads people to disassociate from their bodies and take flight into their minds. In active addiction, the addict uses drugs to escape his problems. In sobriety, he tries to *think* his way through them. Both strategies are essentially reactive.

Yoga is a superior eleventh-step discipline as it helps the addict process challenging emotional states. It also cultivates the capacities of *proprioception* and *interoception*. Proprioception refers to how one receives and interprets information from the musculoskeletal system. Interoception refers to our awareness of visceral stimuli from within the body (Payne; Levine; Crane-Godreau 2015). Yoga, therefore, is an extremely powerful tool for the training of one's attention. When we make slow deliberate movements, we employ the neocortex, one of the most refined areas of brain functioning (Cope 1999). This helps addicts transform habitual thought patterns and emotional reactions. Other benefits include (but are not limited to) decreased heart rate, lowered anxiety, and increased stimulation of the reward centers of the brain. These are just some of the reasons why yoga has been identified as a form of Complementary Alternative Medicine by the National Institutes of Health (Soni 2010).

The twelfth step is about service. AA old timers insisted that service was the real *work* of the steps; that the first 11 Steps merely qualify you to take up the work of the twelfth step. The thinking being that no one has any business telling someone to write an inventory or make amends if he hasn't done it himself. We shouldn't recommend yoga if we don't practice it ourselves. And we shouldn't preach recovery if we are not recovered. *The message is the messenger.*

Recovered addicts have been graced with a powerful gift or *charis* that enables them to serve as instruments in the healing of other addicts. They are *wounded healers*. Their bodies still bear the wound of addiction but their psyches have been healed of the obsession to use. While these realities are largely unknown, ignored, or denied by the clinical world, they are readily understood by theologians, spiritual practitioners, and students of religion.

St. Augustine gave us the concept of *prevenient grace* (prevenient means to "go before"). He argued that the misfortune that brought you to your knees was actually a form of grace—of God acting in your life prior to your conversion. Seen from this perspective, addiction is God's way of commanding our attention. It is God's call. Unfortunately, most addicts refuse His call, time and again, thinking that they can beat the game on their own.

With every refusal the addict's world contracts that much more. Many of us reached a point where our sole freedom lay in the wherewithal to obtain and use drugs. We could no longer work, pay bills, or feed ourselves. All we could do was hustle money to buy drugs. But even then we could say "yes" to God. We say yes the moment we give up. Genuine surrender brings a measure of power that was not there even a moment before. Many addicts report that at some point in the step process "something clicked" and what had seemed impossible suddenly became easy.

Recovery, however, is not an event but a process. We must take the gift and pay it forward. We must perform what John Wesley, the founder of the Methodist church, called acts of *piety* and *mercy*. In the Christian tradition, piety could be anything from worship to fasting to studying scripture. We would identify it with the disciplines we take up in Step 11 (e.g., yoga, meditation, reading spiritual literature). Mercy is service—the twelfth step. Wesley stressed that both were necessary and each complemented the other. If one is too focused on the eleventh step, they run the risk of becoming spiritually self-centered. Their practices are more about feeling good than they are about deepening their relationship with God.

An exclusive concern with the twelfth step can lead to inflation, to the conviction that one is spiritually unique or superior. The addict pursues sponsorship less out of a concern for others than out of a desire for recognition and admiration. We practice the eleventh step, in part, to stay humble.

In Steps 10–12 the pendulum swings back in the direction of power. By this time addicts have recovered and have been empowered to help others. This is the best possible outcome that addicts can achieve. And it has been replicated thousands upon thousands of times since Bill W. had his "hot flash" in Townes Hospital in November 1934. The 12 Steps are still the most powerful modality ever used in the treatment of alcoholism and addiction.

But despite the best efforts of thousands of recovered addicts, the problem continues to morph and grow. Although we can do much to help addicts on an individual basis, we have made no headway in meeting the larger problem. We have long struggled to understand the etiology of addiction. Why is there so much addiction? And why is it getting worse? Before we answer these questions, let us take a brief look at some important dates and trends in the history of addiction.

Before we answer these questions, we must first spend some time exploring 12-Step spirituality and then the history of addiction.

7

SPIRITUAL, NOT RELIGIOUS

Although AA founder Bill Wilson attended a Congregational church in his youth, he was not a religious person as an adult. Prior to his spiritual awakening he thought of himself as an atheist-leaning agnostic. During his active alcoholism, he never entertained the idea that religion or spirituality might be a viable means of recovery. Nor did he become religious as a result of his involvement with the Oxford Group. From the time he got sober until the day he died, Bill Wilson was *spiritual, not religious.*

With that said, imagine his surprise when his old drinking buddy, Ebby Thatcher (1896–1966), told him that he had "gone religious" and joined the Oxford Group. Bill reports that although he was aghast at Ebby's proclamation, he was also intrigued (*Big Book*). So much so that, three days into his last detox, he asked Ebby to visit him in order to take him through the first three Oxford Group exercises (surrender, inventory, and confession). After Ebby left, Bill experienced what he would later call his "hot flash"—an overwhelming encounter with a bright mystical light that left him shaken but also somehow certain that he would never drink again.

His experience, however, was far from reassuring. It was so disorienting that Bill asked the doctor whether he was still sane. It was only after addiction pioneer Dr. William Silkworth reassured and comforted him that he was able to seriously consider the meaning and significance of what he had undergone. (Readers should note that had Silkworth taken a more conservative approach and diagnosed Bill as psychotic, AA may very well have never been born.)

In order to better understand what had happened to him, Bill asked for a copy of William James's *The Varieties of Religious Experience* (*The Varieties*). His reading of this book would not only determine the future of AA and the 12 Steps, it would also exert a profound influence on American culture. Before we discuss why that is so, we should first take a closer look at the spiritual exercises practiced by the Oxford Group.

THE OXFORD GROUP

The Oxford Group exercises have been described differently by different authors. We understand them to have been:

1. Surrender
2. Inventory
3. Confession
4. Restitution
5. Prayer and *Listening*
6. Witnessing

The Oxford Group was an overwhelmingly white and upper middle class fellowship. It was also exclusively Protestant. Upon joining the group, new members were asked to name their sins—those thoughts and behaviors that, although they knew they were wrong, they could not refrain from doing; in other words, those things over which they were *powerless*. Given the Oxford Group's demographic, these behaviors tended to be pretty tame by the standards of most addicts and alcoholics. If they were criminal, they were usually of the white collar variety. However, many Oxford Groupers did confess to things like infidelity, lust, lying, and greed.

After confessing his sinfulness, the new member would get on his knees and say a *Sinner's Prayer*. This marked the beginning of his spiritual journey. Bill would modify and elaborate this exercise into steps one through three. He removed all references to Christ and sin, but added the concepts of powerlessness over alcohol and unmanageability.

Inventory was a written exercise that focused on what were called the *four absolutes*. The four absolutes (distilled from the Sermon on the

Mount in the Gospel of Matthew) were: love, purity, unselfishness, and honesty. Basically, the exercise involved looking at how one fell short of these standards. Do you demonstrate your love for your family or do you take them for granted? Purity dealt with issues surrounding sexuality and/ or money. Unselfishness asked whether one made any substantial sacrifice for the well-being of others. And while it was assumed that everyone would fall short in these three areas, honesty was a different matter. The Oxford Group held its members to a very rigorous standard of honesty. This emphasis is found in the *Big Book* as well. For as we have already noted, Bill is adamant that the only alcoholics who could not recover were those who were "incapable of being honest with themselves" (*Big Book*).

Needless to say, the fourth step bears scant resemblance to the four absolutes. The fourth step addresses resentment, fear, and sexuality. We do not know for certain what prompted Bill to discard the four absolutes but there is strong evidence that the new emphasis on fear was a direct result of his having read the *The Varieties* by philosopher William James. In the chapter called *The Religion of Healthy-Mindedness*, James writes, "But whereas Christian theology has always considered *forwardness* to be the essential vice of this part of human nature, the mind-curers say that the mark of the beast in it is *fear*. . . ." Bill appears to have adopted this idea because the *Big Book* discusses fear at length and never once mentions disobedience or forwardness. Perhaps he recognized that the idea of obedience would not play well with alcoholics. In any case, we do know that Bill was deeply interested in "new thought," otherwise known as "mind cure," a uniquely American movement that holds that sickness ultimately originates in the mind, and that *right thinking* can affect healing. The theme of right thinking appears throughout the *Big Book*. Again and again, Bill challenges the alcoholic to examine his "old ideas" and false beliefs.

The fifth step corresponds to the Oxford Group's practice of confession and the ninth step to restitution. Bill changed the language of step eleven from *prayer and listening* to *prayer and meditation*. Oxford Groupers would join in prayer, followed by a period of silence. It was during this time that they *listened* for the promptings of the Holy Spirit. Many members even kept journals to record what came to them. For example, the journal of Anne Smith (1881–1949)—remembered as the *mother of AA*—was copied and widely circulated among the members of the original fellowship in Akron. It continued to serve as a source of inspiration for recovering alcoholics long after her death. One can only assume that Bill replaced the practice of listening with the more traditional discipline of meditation to avoid alienating the newly sober, especially those from non-Christian backgrounds.

Witnessing morphed into the twelfth step. Oxford Groupers bore witness (or *testified*) to the life-changing effects of their six-step program. Twelve-steppers bear witness to the reality of recovery to the still sick and suffering alcoholic. The Oxford Group has been described as an evangelical-pietist movement. Its members took up specific practices to kindle an *inner light*. That was the pietistic element. Afterwards, they became evangelists and spread the good news of redemption. Likewise, the recovered alcoholic is expected to "carry the message" of recovery to others. The *Big Book* is an evangelical-pietistic text, sans the Christian elements.

Where theologians may understand AA in terms of evangelical pietism, anthropologists might describe it as a charismatic healing cult. It is a movement that began with the dramatic spiritual healing of a single individual. That person, in turn, affected healing in others by his gift—or *charis*. (This is but a variation of the theme of the *wounded healer*.) The term cult should not be understood as a pejorative—a cult or *cultus* simply refers to the ritual and beliefs of a given group. Whether a movement can survive the death of its founder depends on the strength of its organizational structure and whether the experience of the founder can be reliably and consistently replicated in its members. AA has met both challenges, although only a minority of its members actually practice the steps.

WILLIAM JAMES AND *THE VARIETIES OF RELIGIOUS EXPERIENCE*

Bill's experience at the hospital did not result in a conversion to Christianity. However, he would take a deep interest in Christian mystical literature and even went on to receive spiritual direction from Reverend Samuel Moor Shoemaker (1893–1963), famed rector of Calvary Episcopal Church in New York City. But, unlike Dr. Bob, Bill always downplayed AA's Christian origins. He was concerned that AA be accessible to all, regardless of race, creed, or spiritual orientation. His thinking on this matter was shaped both by personal inclination and by his close reading of *The Varieties*.

Few academics or AA members fully appreciate the impact of *The Varieties* on the subsequent development of AA. This is because few in the recovery community actually read the book. William James is regarded by some to be America's greatest thinker. Trained as a physician, he never practiced medicine. Instead, he did seminal work in the fields of psychology, philosophy, psychical research, and religious studies. His book, *The Principles of Psychology*, was a major work. (James was dubbed the "Father of American Psychology.") James and his friend and colleague, Charles Sanders Peirce, created pragmatism, the only properly American school of philosophy. He was also a founder of the American Society for Psychical Research. Far, far ahead of his time, he outlined a theory of mind that allowed for the scientific study of paranormal phenomena. His thought continues to inform research in many areas, including religion, mysticism, and the philosophy of mind. However, it is *The Varieties* that may have had the greatest and most lasting impact on American culture.

James's long years of research led him to conclude that life, and especially human consciousness, was a messy, ambiguous, often contradictory, and deeply mysterious affair. Furthermore, he argued that most people could not face this ambiguity and preferred the certainty afforded by religious dogma, scientific materialism, or political affiliation. And while none of these ideologies could be proven *true* in the strict sense, people embraced them just to avoid the nagging insecurity that resulted from taking an honest stock of the perplexities of life. Humans, therefore, were prone to black and white binary thinking; things were either true or false, right or wrong, or good or bad. James wanted to avoid that trap—he embraced life in all its complexity and diversity. This commitment is what motivated his interest in mysticism and the paranormal.

James's pragmatism meant that he was most interested in the *cash value* of a proposition or belief. He argued that truth is ultimately a matter of practical consequence. The value of a belief lay in its power to help people successfully negotiate the trials and tribulations of daily life. Jamesian pragmatism is a quintessentially American philosophy. Like most Americans, James was impatient with mere speculation—he was interested in what worked.

All of these ideas inform *The Varieties*. James takes a broad view of spiritual experience. He examines the testimony of the great mystics and prophets from many religions over broad spans of time. At the same time, he includes contemporary newspaper accounts of conversions at nearby church revivals. He also relates the healing testimonies of several mind-cure practitioners. James makes no distinction between high or low, good or bad, or true or false religion. Nor is he interested in creed or dogma. He is only concerned with the practical consequences of a given spiritual experience. For James, mystical experiences could only be validated by their *fruits*, and never by their *roots*. Ultimately, it matters little what religion you belong to if it has no bearing on how you treat others. The real question is: did your spiritual experience make you a better person, a more loving parent, or a more considerate friend? He makes a strong argument that a spiritual awakening is of little consequence if it does not enhance the lives of those around you. His is a pragmatic and very democratic approach to religious experience.

James comes to few conclusions at the end of his book. After all, he did not want to simplify a complex and messy phenomenon merely for the sake of intellectual clarity. He did, however, make three bold assertions: (1) that our visible world is part of a more spiritual universe from which it draws its chief significance; (2) that union or harmonious relation with that higher universe is our true end; and (3) that prayer or inner communion with the spirit thereof—be that spirit *God* or *law*—is a process wherein the work is really done, and spiritual energy flows in and produces effects, psychological or material, within the phenomenal world.

Bill read *The Varieties* while still in the hospital shortly after his spiritual experience. Given his state of mind, the book could only have made a profound impression. To recapitulate:

- Bill was not a religious person, nor was he seeking a spiritual experience
- Ebby witnessed to Bill while the latter man was still drinking
- Bill did the exercises of surrender, restitution, and confession while in the hospital
- As a result, he had a profound *psychic change* and never drank again
- Bill read *The Varieties* in order to better understand his experience

Please note that Bill (unlike Dr. Bob) was not seeking a spiritual remedy for his alcoholism. He did not seek it—it found him. Furthermore, he did the exercises in the hospital with his old childhood friend, Ebby. He did not do them in an Oxford Group setting. Finally, his understanding of what happened to him was not determined by the principles and tenets of the Oxford Group but by the philosophy of William James. James, for his part, was explicit in stating his belief that alcoholics could, and often did, find healing through spirituality. He quotes an unknown "medical man," who asserted that, "The only radical remedy I know for dipsomania is religiomania."

SPIRITUALITY, NOT RELIGION

James's emphasis on the effect, rather than the origin, of a spiritual experience made a lasting impression upon Bill. It led him to speculate that, if James was right, he should be able to abstract the Oxford Group exercises from their Christian content so as to make them available to virtually any alcoholic, regardless of religious background. History has vindicated Bill's intuition. AA may be a *para-religious* institution rooted in the Christian tradition, but it is decidedly non-religious. AA members are not bound by any dogma. Members are free to believe or not to believe as they see fit. Twelve-steppers engage in the same practices without necessarily maintaining the same beliefs. This is the difference between orthopraxis (same practice) and orthodoxy (same belief). It is one of the reasons why so many twelve-steppers claim that they are spiritual and not religious.

THE JUNGIAN PERSPECTIVE

Twelve-step spirituality was also influenced by the thought of C. G. Jung (1875–1961). In 1931, a wealthy Rhode Islander named Rowland Hazard was facing institutionalization for his alcoholism. Desperate, he went all the way to Zurich, Switzerland to be treated by Jung. He stayed for several months and by the time he left, felt that he had finally achieved lasting recovery. Much to his chagrin, he found himself drunk in short order. Later, he returned to Jung and asked him why he could not recover. Jung told him that while many alcoholics do recover as a result of "vital spiritual experiences," he never saw someone as bad as Hazard get better. He went on to say that such recoveries appear to involve "huge emotional displacements and rearrangements" where "ideas, emotions, and attitudes that were once the guiding forces of the lives of these men are suddenly cast aside and a completely new set of conceptions and motives begin to dominate them" (*Big Book*). These words prompted Hazard to seek out such an experience, which eventually brought him to the halls of the Oxford Group.

Jung, whose own psychology is profoundly spiritual, did not know of the role he played in the genesis of AA until a few months before his death in 1961. He learned about it as a result of a letter sent by Bill on January 23 of that year. In it Bill wrote, "Very many thoughtful AAs are students of your writings. Because of your conviction that man is something more than intellect, emotion, and two dollars' worth of chemicals, you have especially endeared yourself to us." Toward the end of his letter he says, "You will also be interested to learn that, in addition to the 'spiritual experience,' many AAs report a great variety of psychic phenomena, the cumulative weight of which is very considerable. Other members have—following their recovery in AA—been much helped by your practitioners. A few have been intrigued by the *I Ching* and your remarkable introduction to that work" (D. Schoen, *The War of the Gods in Addiction*). Bill's comments reveal the extent of AA's debt to Jungian psychology and also show the spiritually adventurous side of the early movement. Recovery was conceived of as a spiritual quest. Abstinence was only its beginning.

The refrain of "just don't drink, go to meetings, and ask for help" is worlds apart from AA's original spirit and intent.

Jung's reply is even more remarkable. In a letter dated January 30, he describes alcoholism as a kind of misguided mystical impulse—a "thirst for wholeness" (Schoen). Here Jung is very close to James who wrote, "The sway of alcohol over mankind is unquestionably due to its power to stimulate the mystical faculties of human nature, usually crushed to earth by the cold facts and dry criticisms of the sober hour" (James). He goes on to describe this thirst as an "unrecognized spiritual need" that will lead the individual "into perdition if it is not counteracted by real religious insight or by the protective wall of human community" (Schoen). He believed that the disappearance of genuine religious experience in modern times literally drove people to drink in excess.

Furthermore, he identified the power behind alcoholism as *evil*. He says, "An ordinary man, not protected by an action from above and isolated in society, cannot resist the power of evil, which is called very aptly the Devil" (Schoen). As we have seen, Jung's insistence that the alcoholic cannot get better without the protection of both God and community also lies at the heart of 12-Step philosophy. Bill also argues that recovery is both spiritual and altruistic. And while one does not hear a lot of talk of evil in recovery circles, any addict will tell you that drugs will eventually rob you of everything—money, health, relationships, and ultimately, your life. Viewed from that perspective, addiction is the very picture of evil.

Jungian psychology relates addiction to what it calls the *shadow complex*. As we noted earlier, the shadow is comprised of all those things that one is unwilling to acknowledge about themselves. (It should be noted that repressed trauma can also be constellated in the shadow. The injuries we have suffered at the hands of others are often entangled with our unacknowledged insecurities, pettiness, and rage.) If these forces are never acknowledged they will eventually manifest as symptoms. Sometimes they are felt emotionally, other times they are enacted (or projected) interpersonally. For example, if fear is a major part of my shadow, I might deal with it by bullying others. For if I can make others fear me, then I can delude myself into believing I am fearless. Or if I cannot acknowledge my own jealousy, I will be quick to point it out in others. Over time, the shadow complex can become unbearable. I struggle to present a socially acceptable persona even as my emotions and behaviors are becoming increasingly volatile and uncontrollable. As the tension mounts, I find release by getting high. If nothing changes, I will likely become addicted.

As we have seen, recovery begins with an admission of powerlessness. The addict must take honest stock of their personal condition and surrender control. The addict must reorient away from narrow self-interest and move toward a Higher Power. It's an abstract concept for many and is one that inevitably drives many out of treatment who are not yet ready to ponder the possibility of something larger than themselves. But the reality is, from our experience, spirituality, or a belief in some form of a higher power, is crucial to recovery.

From a Jungian perspective, recovery demands a depth of honesty that goes way beyond admitting one's powerlessness over drugs or alcohol. It requires the addict to finally face the shadow complex that led to substance abuse in the first place.

If the addict takes an honest fourth and fifth step, they will begin to *individuate*. This means that the energy used to repress and hide from the shadow complex is now available for psycho-spiritual growth. With individuation, the addict has begun to move toward "wholeness." Having faced and acknowledged the very worst things about themselves, they can begin to integrate those elements they had repressed or disavowed into their psyche. Jung called this the "marriage of opposites" or the "coincidentia oppositorum." His idea of wholeness had less to do with becoming *good* as it did with becoming *conscious*. If I become aware of what lurks inside me, I will be less likely to project it upon another person.

In 12-Step terms, this greater consciousness or new awareness is what lets us know when we are "off the beam" and need to write inventory or make amends. Twelve-steppers would be well advised to take stock of Jung's approach. Too often, the steps are looked upon as a kind of master self-improvement program. And while they can go a long way toward helping an addict learn to forgive and cultivate healthy behaviors and relationships, it is all too easy to become unrealistic about what it means to be in recovery. The steps do not lead to perfection nor do they guarantee personal success or happiness. Instead, they enable the addict to embrace life, with all its trials and hardships. It is not about what I can get or how I look. It is about being of service to God and to others.

Individuation is the means by which we come to know God. Jung holds that one cannot know God without first confronting the shadow. And individuation, like recovery, is about much more than one's personal development. Jung believed that individuation was of great value to the wider world. For if I integrate my shadow, I will be less likely to project it onto (and thereby harm) others. If I lead a more authentic life, I will come to feel myself to be a part of something much greater than the small orbit of my fantasies and desires. As I become more conscious, I will also become more aware of the needs and feelings of others.

MORAL PSYCHOLOGY

Bill Wilson had a strong sense of posterity. He rightly imagined that the *Big Book* would be read and studied long after he was gone. He was also keenly aware that his thesis that spirituality was the key to recovery was bound to be provocative and controversial and might even be perceived as a threat to the medical establishment. Therefore, Bill buttressed his argument by appealing to the authority of Jung and James. He also cited his attending physician, Dr. William D. Silkworth (1873–1951). Silkworth may not have had the same exalted status as the others, but he was a prominent figure in his own era. Like James and Jung, he believed that alcoholics could be healed by spiritual means.

Silkworth wrote, "We doctors have realized for a long time that some sort of moral psychology was of urgent importance to alcoholics, but its application presented difficulties beyond our conception" (*Big Book*). Twelve-steppers are usually taught that *moral psychology* is just another term for spirituality. And while that is basically true, moral psychology also refers to a specific era in the history of American psychology.

Moral psychology emerged in the late 18th century in response to the barbaric treatment of the insane in American mental asylums. In that era, patients were "treated" with beatings, blisterings, and all manner of psychological abuse. In 1796, a group of New York Quakers, led by William Tuke, took matters into their own hands and opened the first facility, or home, that followed the principles of what they called "moral treatment." Rooted in Quaker religious belief and practice, moral treatment emphasized kindness and gentleness. Patients were looked upon as brethren, rather than as defective or broken. Programming revolved around art and education. Much time was spent outdoors, working in the gardens or taking long walks. Patients were fed four times a day and given ample free time for reading, writing, playing chess, or reciting poetry. Tea parties were a frequent occurrence and clients were even encouraged to dress formally (R. Whitaker, *Mad in America*).

The ideas and practices that undergird moral psychology were widely adopted and practiced until the 1840s. While many patients did not respond, there were also many stunning successes. Its downfall was the result of several factors. One was the massive expansion of the asylum system across the United States. The size of these facilities made it impossible to replicate the homelike atmosphere that was an integral aspect of moral psychology. Furthermore, it was an expensive form of treatment that few states could afford to implement.

In the end, moral psychology came to be regarded as a hopelessly naïve and unscientific treatment modality. The field of neurology, which rose to prominence in the aftermath of the Civil War, insisted that mental illnesses were brain diseases that demanded medical treatment. Practitioners of moral psychology, with their old-fashioned Christian beliefs, were regarded as embarrassingly anachronistic by the larger medical and scientific communities. Once again the pendulum swung back toward pathologization. For a brief period, the emotionally disturbed were welcomed and embraced by the larger community. Patients who were suffering from mania, psychosis, or alcoholism were still viewed as full members of the human family. But by the turn of the 20th century, with the rise of social Darwinism and the eugenics movement, addicts were again treated as outcasts—defective creatures whose very existence posed a dangerous threat to the country's gene pool.

As we will see in the upcoming text, moral psychology anticipates many of the insights of Dislocation Theory. They both understand spirituality in relational terms. Spirituality is realized in acts of kindness, gentleness, compassion, and love. Both moral psychology and Dislocation Theory insist that one can only truly heal in a warm and welcoming community, and that shunning and labeling will never serve the cause of wellness.

HARDWIRED FOR SPIRITUAL EXPERIENCE

George Vaillant is a prominent contemporary thinker whose work can help us better understand the biological correlates of spiritual experience. His book, *Spiritual Evolution*, is a must read for anyone interested in the relationship between recovery and spirituality. Its central thesis is that we are *hardwired* for spiritual experience—that our very bodies are designed to feel love, compassion, forgiveness, and empathy. However, he shows that these feelings depend on social context. Humans must create favorable conditions for them to grow. Stress, trauma, and conflict inhibit their growth. We must learn how to skillfully create conditions if we are to realize the "angels of our better nature."

Vaillant is an MD and former nonalcoholic trustee of AA. After many years of studying recovery, he came to identify four factors that he believed were essential to recovery: external supervision, ritualized dependency on a competing behavior, new love relationships, and deepened spirituality (Vaillant). Addicts need supervision because they do not know what to do. They need the steady hand of an experienced sponsor who can help negotiate the rough waters of early recovery. Attending meetings and taking up disciplines like prayer and meditation serve as *competing behaviors* against addiction. Love relationships are imperative. On the one hand, the recovering addict must feel cared for—on the other, he must develop compassionate bonds with those addicts he is trying to help. Recovering addicts must also engage in spiritual practices to find a measure of serenity. One of the central themes of this book is that addicts cannot recover if they do not learn how to regulate stress and focus their attention.

Finally, Vaillant shows that the brain chemistry for both attachment and addiction is essentially the same. He details how drugs and alcohol stimulate dopamine release in the nucleus acumens, which is a core part of the brain's reward circuitry. Alcohol also decreases excitation of the amygdala which lessens fear and guilt (Vaillant). Mother-child attachment also diminishes amygdala firing while, at the same time, increasing dopamine and endorphin production. Loving attachment also results in the release of oxytocin, popularly known as the *love drug*. Vaillant's data shows that connection is indeed the antidote to addiction. When we are in the company of those who care about us, we become more relaxed. Our bodies produce chemicals (endorphins, dopamine, and oxytocin) that produce feelings of pleasure and love. We are literally wired for these experiences. We only turn to artificial means of getting them when they are not readily available. This means that Americans are turning to opiates and other drugs because we are not having these experiences with our friends and families or in our homes, schools, and workplaces. Vaillant's work strongly supports the premises of Dislocation Theory.

We hope that the reader can now better appreciate the genius of the 12 Steps. They heal where other modalities fail, largely because they understand that recovery cannot occur in isolation, that it must involve both the mending of old relationships and the establishment of new ones. Recent research in neurobiology has further enhanced our understanding of the pivotal role of interpersonal relationships for addicts in early recovery. We are also beginning to understand how healing from stress and trauma enables meaningful connection. The pieces of the puzzle are finally coming together.

Those of us who have found lasting recovery owe a great debt to Bill Wilson. His adoption of James's pluralistic approach to spirituality made the steps accessible to people from virtually any religious background. Today there are many flourishing 12-step Buddhist sanghas. There is also White Bison, a 12-step movement that has recontextualized the steps to make them more culturally appropriate for Native Americans and indigenous peoples generally. There are 12-step yogis and 12-step contemplatives. Most addicts feel free to explore any of the world's many wisdom traditions.

Bill's friend, the author and philosopher Aldous Huxley (1894–1963), called Wilson the "greatest social architect" of the 20th century. He believed the steps to be a prime example of what he called the "perennial philosophy." Huxley argued that all human discord and discontent ultimately arose as a result of being disconnected from the source—whether one calls it Atman, Allah, or God. The word *religion* is derived from the Latin verb *religare*, which means *to tie* or *to bind*. One engages in spiritual practices so as to bind oneself to God, to reconnect with *the source*. Huxley believed that alcoholism was symptomatic of spiritual disconnection.

AA has a rich and varied history. It was shaped by James and Jung and later endorsed by Huxley and Vaillant. Unfortunately, few doctors or academics have taken note of its supporters or its pedigree. Despite its cultural prominence, it has been consistently marginalized by the medical and academic establishments.

Now, let's take a brief look at some important dates and trends in the history of addiction.

8

DATES AND TRENDS

If we are to understand how we got here then we should take stock, at least a bit, of where we have been. There are many writings from antiquity and the middle ages that warn against the overconsumption of alcohol. Drinking by oneself was thought to cause a *hardening of the soul*. However, the demonization of alcohol and of those who imbibe—the prohibition mentality—only began to take hold after alcoholism became a widespread social problem in Great Britain (i.e., the *gin craze*) in the 1700s.

1784 saw the birth of the temperance movement in the United States. It began with Benjamin Rush's book, *An Inquiry into the Effects of Ardent Spirits upon the Human Body and Mind*. In it, Rush warned against the overconsumption of alcohol and advised moderation.

The first widely used spiritual methods for treating alcoholism originated with Native Americans, the most famous being the *Code of Handsome Lake*. In 1799, a dissolute 65-year-old Seneca Indian named Handsome Lake had a near death experience after drinking whiskey for several days. Upon returning to consciousness he reported that the Great Spirit had instructed him to teach the people to abstain from alcohol, honor the ancestors and traditions, and treat women with respect. For over 200 years the Code of Handsome Lake has been followed by thousands of Native Americans and has shown itself to be a highly effective recovery modality. (Note: Bill Wilson's experience mirrors that of Handsome Lake in significant ways. Both men became *charismatic healers* after encountering a spiritual being during a *near death* experience.)

The term *alcoholism* was coined in 1849 by Swedish physician Magnus Huss. He was the first person to explicitly identify addiction to alcohol as a disease. Prior to that it was known as *dipsomania* and was understood to be a "morbid craving for alcohol."

TIMELINE

- 1861–1865: Widespread opioid addiction was documented for the first time in the United States during the Civil War.
- 1864: The first *Inebriate Asylum* opened in New York to warehouse those afflicted with *alcoholic insanity*.
- 1893: Methamphetamine was synthesized for the first time in Japan.
- 1898: Bayer marketed a new *nonaddictive* alternative to morphine called *heroin*. From 1898–1910 heroin was sold and used as a pain reliever and cough suppressant.
- Early 1900s: There was speculation that alcoholism may have been due to what is now called *seasonal affective disorder*. Around this same time, addicts and alcoholics were being put into bromide induced comas—the belief being that the coma itself would act as a cure. Many addicts died as a result of this *treatment*. This would be tried again in 1927, except this time patients would be put into *insulin* comas.
- 1907: Several states, under the influence of the eugenics movement, passed laws that forbade marriage to those suffering from addiction. There is some evidence that sterilizations were also performed.
- 1908: President Theodore Roosevelt appointed Hamilton Wright to be the nation's first *Opium Commissioner*. Wright called Americans *the greatest drug fiends in the world*.
- 1913: California became the first state to enact a cannabis prohibition law.
- 1914: Saw passage of the Harrison Act, a federal law that regulated and taxed the production, importation, and distribution of opiates and coca products. This made it illegal for doctors to prescribe opiates to treat opiate addiction. Passage of the Harrison Act proved to be a boon for organized crime and especially for

Arnold Rothstein (variously nicknamed *The Brain, The Fixer,* and *Mr. Big*). Rothstein, who is most famous for conspiring to fix the 1919 World Series, was the principal financier of the international heroin trade from 1914 until his murder in 1928.

Rates of alcoholism spiked during WWI, especially in those countries directly involved in the war. In 1914, Russian Tsar Nicholas II banned vodka and shut down Russia's 400-plus distilleries. The ban was in reaction to a marked increase of alcohol consumption in the military. Alcoholism had spread through the ranks during the Russian-Japanese war in 1904 and again at the onset of WWI.[1]

The Russian ban on vodka was a spectacular failure. In a foreshadowing of what would soon occur in the United States, citizens distilled their own vodka and a thriving black market emerged, rife with violence, crippling alcoholism, and widespread health problems. During the same era, England tried to crack down on alcohol abuse by cutting the number of pub licenses, limiting their business hours, increasing penalties for drunkenness, and hiking taxes on booze. None of it had the desired effect.

Alcohol abuse also soared in the United States during WWI; this helped fuel the temperance movement and eventually led to legal prohibition. From 1920 to 1933 there was a nationwide ban on the production, consumption, transport, sale, and import of alcoholic beverages. As in Russia, the ban created a flourishing black market and underground culture of speakeasies and criminal enterprises that produced and sold booze.

The bootlegging industry was famously violent—the national murder rate rose by 78 percent during the first 10 years of prohibition. There was a marked increase in political corruption and overall crime; gangsters from Chicago to New York to Los Angeles grew enormously rich and powerful throughout the 1920s and early 1930s.[2]

Prohibition also led people to drink anything containing alcohol, including paint, cleaning products, and other harmful chemicals. There are estimates that more than 10,000 people died from drinking harmful chemicals during this era, but the number is likely far higher.[3]

Criminalization led bootleggers to increase the potency of their product. For the most part, they did not make wine or beer. Instead, they distilled high-proof moonshine that could be diluted by retailers. (We see this same trend with illegal drugs. Addicts have moved from ritalin to adderall to crystal meth. The THC content of marijuana is several times higher than it was in the 1970s. Opiate addicts have progressed from OxyContin to heroin to fentanyl.)

Today, alcohol is one of the top moneymakers in the American economy with sales of more than $235 billion in 2017. The social costs of drinking remain high since a large portion of crime is alcohol-related, including drunken driving, domestic violence, assault, rape, and murder. A 2005 study found that alcohol abuse cost the U.S. economy more than $220 billion per year in lost productivity.

The 1930s was the era of *reefer madness*. Poverty and unemployment led to widespread hostility toward immigrants and foreigners. Cannabis use was identified with Latinos, especially with people of Mexican descent. Harry Anslinger, commissioner of the Federal Bureau of Narcotics (precursor of the Drug Enforcement Agency), told the public that smoking marijuana led to insanity, criminality, and death. Passage of the Marihuana Tax Act in 1937 made it illegal to possess or sell the drug.

- June 10, 1935: The birth of Alcoholics Anonymous.
- 1935: Shadel Sanatorium began using aversion therapy. This modality tried to discourage drinking by associating liquor consumption with negative consequences. It is the theory underlying the use of disulfiram, or antabuse.
- 1948–1952: Many addicts and alcoholics were lobotomized (lobotomies were medical procedures that severed connections to the prefrontal cortex). At the time, it was believed that addiction was due to a pathology of the prefrontal cortex. (Tom Waits was right when he said that he'd "rather have a bottle in front of me than a frontal lobotomy.") The 1950s also saw the widespread use of electroshock therapy on addicts and alcoholics. Throughout the 1950s and '60s, LSD was researched as a possible treatment for alcoholism. Of late, there has been a resurgence of interest in the use of psychedelics to treat addiction. Studies are currently being conducted in the United States and abroad.

- 1970: LSD and marijuana were designated Schedule 1 substances, the most restrictive category, reserved for drugs thought to have no medical benefit and the highest potential for abuse.
- 1971: New York opened the first state-sponsored methadone clinic. Until 2010, methadone clinics were the only entities who could legally prescribe narcotics to opiate addicts. (Methadone clinics are an exception to the Harrison Act.)
- 1974–1996: Federal law recognized addiction as a form of disability; many addicts received welfare (and later, disability) benefits for their condition. This ended around the time of welfare reform. However, the overwhelming majority of addicts kept their benefits by getting one or more secondary psychiatric diagnoses. From 1996 to 1998, social security disability enrollment increased by 400%. Applicants were told that they had to be medically compliant if they were to keep their benefits. Since then, substance abuse treatment has become increasingly medicalized despite the relative inefficacy of pharmaceutical interventions.
- 1985 and 1986: Marked the beginning of the crack epidemic. Prior to that time cocaine cost roughly $2,000 an ounce. Supply increased dramatically with the advent of crack; this brought the price down to roughly $600 an ounce. (The price has held steady for over thirty years.) Price deflation is a generalized trend—over the last forty years, illegal drugs have gotten much cheaper even as they become more potent. For example, in 2012 crystal meth cost roughly $1,100 an ounce, today the same amount can be purchased for anywhere between $250 and $450.
- 1986: The Reagan administration acknowledged that the Contra Rebels (supported by the United States and dubbed *freedom fighters* by the president) fighting in Nicaragua received funds that were obtained through cocaine trafficking. Later that year the Kerry Committee determined that U.S. funds that had been earmarked for humanitarian assistance for the Contras had been used as payment to drug traffickers.
- 1994: Marked the beginning of the current crystal meth epidemic. Twenty metric tons of the drug were consumed in 2000—by 2005

that number had increased to 85 metric tons. In 2010 U.S. Customs and Border Protection seized 8,900 pounds of meth; that figure jumped to nearly 82,000 pounds in 2018.[4]

- Mid-1990s: The American Pain Society aggressively pushed the idea that pain should be recognized as the fifth vital sign.

- 1996: Gary Webb published his *Dark Alliance* series in the San Jose Mercury News. The series detailed the sudden appearance of crack cocaine in south-central Los Angeles. Webb maintained that Contra trafficking was a major factor in the genesis of the *crack epidemic*. His claim that the Contra drug dealing may have enjoyed the support and protection of the CIA caused public outrage. Webb's assertions are widely debated to this day. However, it should be noted that in 1998 a CIA internal investigation acknowledged that the agency had covered up Contra drug smuggling activity for over a decade.

- 1996: Purdue Pharma marketed OxyContin as a nonaddictive painkiller.

- 1996: The Veterans Administration designated pain as the fifth vital sign.

- 1996: The beginning of the current opioid epidemic (see Figure 8.1).

- 2000: Congress passed the Drug Addiction Treatment Act. This act effectively circumvented the Harrison Act since it allows any qualified physician to treat narcotic addiction with opioids.

- 2001: The Joint Commission on Accreditation of Healthcare Organizations adopted pain as the fifth vital sign as a standard.

- 2002: The FDA approved buprenorphine for the treatment of opiate addiction. (Buprenorphine is an opioid medication, a *mixed opioid agonist—antagonist*. Suboxone is a combination of buprenorphine and naloxone.)

- Between 2008 and 2012: Adderall prescriptions increased threefold.[5]

- 2013: Suboxone sales reach 1.2 billion.[6]

- From 2013 to 2014: There was a 9% increase in the number of fentanyl overdose deaths. Since 2000 there has been a 200% increase in the overall rate of opioid overdose deaths.[7]

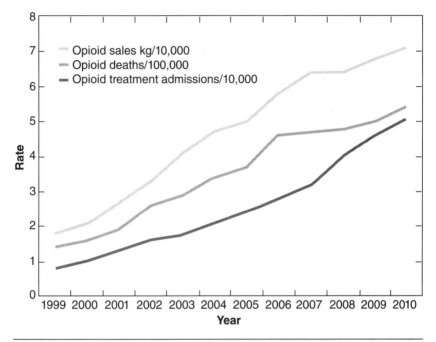

Figure 8.1 Opioid sales, deaths, and treatment admissions[8]

SUMMARY

The timeline speaks for itself. Addiction has ravaged American society, especially over the past fifty years. It is a sordid tale of cynical exploitation, horrifyingly inhumane *treatment*, institutional corruption, and criminalization.

So here we are now, with an opioid crisis wiping out more Americans in each of two successive years (2016 and 2017) than were lost in the entire Vietnam War. Political leaders and policymakers promise us that we're going to beat this thing. But we don't stand a chance the way we are going.

With every other public health crisis, the government deploys every available resource. We had an ebola outbreak. Five people got ebola. One man died. The response? Hundreds of millions of dollars in emergency funding were released to attack the problem. But when 70,000 people die of drug overdoses, we get a lot of talk and the continual recycling of a bunch of tired ideas. Where's the help? Where's the emergency funding? Our friends, families, and neighbors are dying. They deserve more than lip service.

Until now, the recovery community and their friends and families have looked toward government, law enforcement, and the medical profession for help. But none of those institutions have met the challenge. We believe that's largely because of avarice. The real power lies with the people who have recovered.

We have to stop looking to others for answers and realize that *we are the answer.* We can't bring the addiction epidemic to an end overnight, but we can begin to turn this thing around. The more people we get well, the more people will get well. It's that simple—a healthy pyramid scheme.

We have to grow a movement that's so well-informed, widespread, and dynamic that it can force change. And we must act with urgency. We need boots on the ground and in the trenches; seconds and inches can be the difference between life and death.

But we must remember that we are fighting a war against a well-funded opponent. The drug trade—legal and illegal—is an economic leviathan. Marketing geniuses run the industry, whether they work for powerful corporations like Purdue Pharma or any one of the international criminal cartels.

One would think that the market must be close to being saturated, that the demand for drugs is bound to come down. We doubt it. People stay on opiates for years or even decades. Meanwhile, the growing despair and alienation that plagues our communities is getting worse and worse. Until that changes, people will continue to seek relief and escape.

For the last 20+ years, tens of thousands of addicts have been sent to prison for long sentences on "possession with intent to distribute" convictions. In reality, most of these folks are just addicts who do a little dealing to support their habits. Most people doing time on drug convictions are addicts or users, not dealers. Incarcerating addicts has had virtually no impact on the importation or abuse of illegal drugs.

On the other hand, you have executives of major drug companies who are guilty of far worse, who make millions off of the misery of addicts—and yet none of them are going to jail. In 2007, after a gut-wrenching trial at a federal court in rural Virginia, three Purdue Pharma executives pleaded guilty to misdemeanor charges of *misbranding* OxyContin and were sentenced to three years probation and ordered to perform 400 hours of community service at drug treatment facilities (*New York Times*, July 21, 2007).

In 2007, the company was charged by the Department of Justice and pleaded guilty to fraudulent marketing of OxyContin and paid a $360 million fine. No executives from the Connecticut-based company nor any members of the Sackler family—worth a collective $14 billion—were charged (*Forbes*, July 1, 2015). Countless lives were lost as a result of their actions, yet the penalties they suffered were far less severe than what a working-class addict gets for possession with intent to distribute.

For Purdue Pharma, those fines were nothing more than the cost of doing business. And business has been good. Very good.

NOTES

1. https://www.rbth.com/arts/2014/08/18/when_the_tsar_banned_booze_37603
2. https://www.alcoholproblemsandsolutions.org/effects-of-prohibition/
3. https://vinepair.com/articles/government-prohibition-poison-alcohol/
4. https://www.cnn.com/2018/09/26/health/meth-overdoses-increase-oklahoma-mexico-superlabs/index.html)
5. https://www.psychologytoday.com/us/blog/where-science-meets-the-steps/201805/will-adderall-be-the-new-opioid-crisis
6. https://www.thefix.com/content/hard-to-kick-suboxone?page=all
7. https://www.cdc.gov/mmwr/preview/mmwrhtml/mm6450a3.htm
8. CDC (Cent. Dis. Control Prev.). 2011. Vital signs: overdoses of prescription opioid pain relievers—United States, 1999–2008. MMWR 60: 1487–92.

9

THE DISLOCATION THEORY OF ADDICTION

There is a world of misunderstanding about what addiction actually is and what it tells us about ourselves. We have already talked a bit about how addiction relates to a lack of connection. Substance abuse is symptomatic of a much deeper problem. A problem that is physical, spiritual, and *social* in nature.

It is time that we come together and really examine this phenomena from multiple perspectives. The 12-Step movement has brought recovery to millions, but we now need to reach out to people beyond the confines of the various fellowships. We need to cultivate new relationships. It is imperative that we connect with parents, academics, clergy, clinicians, and members of the law enforcement community. We must also form common cause with like-minded activists, especially those from the worlds of mental health and criminal justice reform. We need to work tirelessly to educate and enlist new members into our movement. To meet a problem of this magnitude, we need the help of people from every walk of life.

LOSS OF COMMUNITY

To understand why we need to form such a tribe, we must first take an honest look at the reality of life in the United States, especially as it relates to stress and societal decline. The current crisis has been brewing for decades. The fact that it has something to do with a loss of community is amply evident. Most people over the age of 40 would agree that they had more meaningful conversations with family members and friends 10 years ago than they do today. And they would also concur that their confidence in the government, the media, and the medical establishment has sharply declined over that same period. Indeed, American optimism has all but vanished and we are increasingly anxious about the future.

Today, people are born into what Dr. Bruce Alexander calls *dislocation*. Unlike our ancestors or those who were born into intact indigenous cultures, we were raised in a society that had already begun to unravel under the relentless pressures of modernity. We have never had the sense of purpose, belonging, and meaning that defined pre-modern-day cultures. We no longer enjoy the security of strong familial bonds and shared spiritual tradition.

Brick-and-mortar neighborhoods have all but vanished. People no longer shop, congregate, or visit *Main Street*. Neighbors used to be part of one's extended family. Now if someone knocks on the door we think, "Who the hell is that?" We no longer know our neighbors' names.

DIGITAL DANGERS

Digital culture is only exacerbating our sense of alienation. The world is indeed more *connected* because of the internet and social media. We have access to information and people like never before. But it has come at the expense of authentic personal connection. Ironically, this attempt to connect us all—globally and digitally—has led to us all becoming more isolated than ever before.

Life is increasingly virtual. We live in an age of online celebrity, blogebrity, and internet personality. Adults are tethered to their smartphones, whether for work or to stay in constant touch with family and friends. Facebook, Instagram, and Twitter have become the primary source of community for many people. It's where they go for validation, to have their voices heard, or to find out what's going on in the world or even in their own neighborhood. We are far more likely to text, Snap, Tweet,

Instagram, or Facebook than actually sit down and share space with each other. Share time together. Share conversation. Share silence. Human interaction is increasingly disembodied.

STRESS AND ALIENATION

At the same time, many Americans are feeling the effects of unrelenting economic uncertainty—the ever-rising costs of living and higher education, stagnant wages, and the offshoring of jobs. Millennial men will be the first generation of American men who can reasonably expect to earn less than their fathers.

While the opioid epidemic is the most glaring effect, it's certainly not the only symptom of our societal malaise. Things are getting worse across the board—suicide, homelessness, mass incarceration, ecological disaster. Taken together, all of these factors are making life in 21st-century America increasingly untenable. The hard truth is that millions of our fellow citizens lead lives of quiet desperation.

Although we're born with the same innate capacities of our ancestors, we are effectively divorced from the natural world and no longer live in tight-knit extended communities. Humans are social creatures and strong communal ties benefit everyone. Unfortunately, we have not really adapted to modernity. We have the same need for connection that our ancestors had 1,000 years ago, but we now find ourselves struggling to relate to one another in an increasingly fragmented world. The pace of life is relentless and disorienting. We are at the mercy of the gods of Wall Street and Silicon Valley.

Given the anxious lifestyle just described, it is no wonder that addiction has become a pandemic. Alexander argues that addiction is actually an adaptive response. In the face of overwhelming stress and alienation, we turn to substances or other compulsive behaviors to soothe our overwrought minds and bodies. This is what must be thoroughly studied and discussed. The 12 Steps must be recontextualized in light of Dislocation Theory. This is what our movement is all about.

UNDERSTANDING DISLOCATION THEORY

Alexander formulated the Dislocation Theory of Addiction over the course of his career as professor of psychology at Simon Fraser University. His book, *The Globalization of Addiction: A Study in Poverty of the Spirit*, is a magisterial work that is radically transforming our understanding of addiction and recovery. In it, Alexander redefines addiction as any "overwhelming involvement with a substance or an activity that is harmful to oneself or one's social relations."

It is important to note that Alexander does not confine his analysis to the abuse of substances, nor does he medicalize the issue. He argues that one can be *overwhelmingly involved* with any number of behaviors as well. These include (but are not confined to) shopping, working out, eating, sex, or gambling. (The so-called *process addictions*.) By this definition an addict is someone whose investment of time, energy, and/or money in said substance or activity comes at the expense of his parenting, marriage, or work performance.

Dislocation Theory rests upon three interconnected ideas:

1. Psychosocial integration is necessary to well-being
2. Globalizing free markets undermines psychosocial integration
3. Addiction is an adaptive response to sustained dislocation

Alexander's addiction research began with heroin addicts in Vancouver's notorious Downtown Eastside in the 1970s. His findings led him to conduct his now famous *Rat Park* experiments. Before his landmark research, opiate addiction had been widely studied by isolating individual rats in small *skinner boxes* equipped with a button that, when pressed, delivered a hit of morphine to the rat. Not surprisingly, the rats repeatedly hit the button and, in short order, became addicted. Some used to the point of fatal overdose.

Alexander took note of the oppressive, isolated, lonely environment and changed it accordingly. He constructed a large Rat Park replete with toys, food, and other rats. The rats were curious. They explored their environment. They interacted with one another. Remarkably, morphine consumption dropped precipitously and none of the rats became addicted.

Substance abuse largely extinguished itself after the rats were integrated into a safe communal environment.

Following developmental psychologist Erik Erikson, Alexander maintains that emotional well-being is a function of psychosocial integration and communal interdependence—a healthy balance between individual autonomy and communal identity. Alexander describes it as a "profound interdependence between individual and society that normally grows and develops throughout each person's life span. Psychosocial integration reconciles people's vital needs for social belonging with their equally vital needs for individual autonomy and achievement. Psychosocial integration is as much an inward experience of identity and meaning as a set of outward social relationships."

The importance of psychosocial integration was recognized by Charles Darwin. Identified as the *social instinct*, Darwin posited that a tribe with greater social cohesion had a better chance of survival than those that were less integrated. The value of psychosocial integration for individual well-being has been stressed by many other prominent thinkers, including Abraham Maslow, Albert Einstein, and Carl Jung. Its absence is likely a determining factor in the etiology of any number of emotional and stress-related disorders. Alexander argues that addiction only arises in response to a lack of integration or dislocation. That was the case with his rats.

The strength of Alexander's thesis lies in his extensive anthropological and historical research. He shows that addiction only occurs in the wake of the trauma of dislocation. And dislocation, in turn, is usually due to some form of economic or politically motivated violence (e.g., appropriation, exploitation, or neglect). His research shows that addiction in its modern form made its first appearance in the years leading up to the industrial revolution in Great Britain. It first occurred as a result of the massive social change that followed the imposition of the *enclosure acts*.

For hundreds of years, the majority of the English peasant population depended upon a system of shared assets known as the *commons*. Though estates were technically *owned* by a Lord, the peasants were allowed to live off of the land. Life on the commons was communal. Everyone shared resources and the responsibilities of managing the land. This way of life was destroyed by the demands of the market economy. With the emergence of the textile industry, the majority of the peasants were forcibly evicted so more land could be dedicated to producing wool. The loss of long-held traditions and deeply rooted social structures had devastating consequences. Masses of people were forced to move into crowded city slums where poverty, prostitution, disease, and alcoholism ran rampant. Conditions only worsened with the advent of the industrial revolution. The British government would eventually have to resort to mass imprisonment and violence to suppress the poor. These changes were chronicled by many writers, most notably Charles Dickens in the 19th century.

Alexander also compares and contrasts the emergence of alcoholism among the First Nations of Canada with that of Native Americans in the United States. In the United States, alcoholism quickly took hold in the wake of mass extermination, the smallpox epidemic, and the theft of traditional homelands. In Canada, the dislocation of the First Nations peoples was not nearly so quick or dramatic. The inhospitable Canadian climate and landscape served to leave most Northern tribes relatively unmolested. For almost two centuries they were left alone to pursue their traditional way of life. It was only in the 1960s that tribes like the Innu began to suffer the effects of widespread alcoholism. Here again, dislocation was an effect of economic interests—for it was only after their lands had been reappraised in light of their mineral and hydroelectric value that these tribes were forced onto reservations.

The enduring struggles of the Shuswap Indians of Alkali Lake, British Columbia, show the destructive power of sustained dislocation. Throughout the 1950s, '60s, and early '70s, the adult and adolescent population had an alcoholism rate of nearly 100%. By 1979, following the establishment of AA, a deliberate return to traditional culture, and the enforcement of prohibition, those numbers fell by 98%. However, because they were unable to address the long-term effects of dislocation (intergenerational trauma), many of their children and grandchildren have since become alcoholic.

Alexander also cites a landmark study from the 1970s that researched heroin addiction among American soldiers who saw combat in Vietnam. In May of 1972, U.S. congressmen Robert Steele of Connecticut and

Morgan Murphy of Illinois traveled to Vietnam for an official visit. Upon their return they reported that 15% of U.S. troops were addicted to heroin.

The news caused widespread public furor. President Nixon responded by creating The Special Action Office of Drug Abuse Prevention—the federal government's first attempt at targeting drug addiction. Nixon also wanted to track drug-addicted soldiers after they returned to the states to see whether they continued to abuse heroin. A psychiatrist named Dr. Lee Robins was given free reign to set up a program that would test every soldier for heroin after he/she returned to the states.

The results were highly counterintuitive and rather shocking. Dr. Robins found that only about 5% of the soldiers continued to abuse heroin after coming home. This contradicted the widespread expectation that they would remain captive to the *demon drug*. Robins concluded that the low level of relapse was due to the fact that once they were stateside, the soldiers were free from the chaos, depression, and fear produced by the war.

"I think that most people accept that the change in environment—and the fact that the addiction occurred in this exotic environment—makes it plausible that the addiction rate would be that much lower," stated Nixon appointee Jerome Jaffe, who oversaw the study.[1]

Dislocation is a relative condition. The addicted soldiers were able to get off of heroin because they traded a highly dislocated environment (the battlefields of Vietnam) for one that was relatively integrated. They returned to a United States that, despite its political and social unrest, was far less dislocated than the country we live in today.

Dislocation in 21st-century America is accelerating because of relentless economic forces (i.e., free trade and automation) that are utterly indifferent to the well-being of our communities and to the planet itself. In the age of globalization, corporations continually seek ways to maximize profit for shareholders. This is usually accomplished by cutting labor and manufacturing costs. High unemployment is desirable since it drives down labor costs even further. Although these policies benefit stockholders, owners, and upper management, they also cause widespread harm to workers and their families. Globalization has caused a degree of income inequality not seen since the Gilded Age.

Since the adoption of NAFTA and other *free trade* policies, the United States has seen a dramatic contraction of the middle class. Factories have been permanently shuttered. Manufacturing jobs have either disappeared or now require advanced specialized training. Giant buildings that once buzzed with activity sit empty in many cities across America.

Detroit, Flint, Lawrence (MA), Cedar Rapids, Allentown, Buffalo, Cleveland, Newark, and Baltimore—these once-thriving manufacturing hubs are fossils from another era, the detritus of globalization. Their skeletal remains lie crumbling and decaying, the rusted blight of past glory. The destruction of legitimate local economies fuels the black market at home, which is dominated by the sale of illicit drugs. The burgeoning drug trade is, in large part, an effect of the dislocation caused by economic globalization.

Remarkably, researchers have almost never taken the socio-economic dimension of addiction into account. The medical model tacitly endorses the myth of the demon drug—the assumption that addiction is caused by addictive substances. Certain substances have been deemed so addictive that they must be criminalized. This myth lies at the root of the prohibition mentality as well as the *Just Say No, DARE,* and *Scared Straight* campaigns. (All of these fear tactics and propaganda campaigns have been spectacular failures.)

The demon drug narrative also promotes the idea that only *vulnerable* (i.e., defective) individuals become addicted. Instead of looking at social factors, it focuses almost exclusively on biological causation. The dominant narrative asserts that addiction occurs when genetically vulnerable individuals recklessly abuse dangerous substances. If that were the case then there certainly is something genetically distinctive about people living in the United States, Canada, Western Europe, Australia, and Russia—because rates of addiction are markedly higher in those regions than they are in the rest of the world. We contend that those populations suffer high rates of addiction because of dislocation and not because they are more genetically vulnerable than people living elsewhere.

Perhaps Alexander's most stunning revelation is that intact indigenous cultures never suffered from the type of widespread addiction we see in 21st-century America. His research shows that addiction is not a human universal but is actually socially conditioned. In traditional cultures, bonds of kinship, ritual, and shared spiritual belief appear to have served a prophylactic function relative to addiction. Widespread alcoholism arrived in the wake of colonization; indigenous peoples only became addicted after everything that had afforded them a sense of connection and meaning had been either stolen or destroyed.

Here are three features common to most traditional cultures that are conspicuously absent in contemporary American society:

1. Social integration across the life span
2. A shared cosmology
3. Complex resonance with the Earth

Traditional cultures are mindful of the well-being of future generations. They understand that the future depends upon the wise nurturance of children. They also recognize that it *takes a village* to raise a child. These attitudes stand in sharp contrast to our assumption that child-rearing is the exclusive responsibility of the child's biological parents. This has become a major stressor in our society since most adults have to devote the bulk of their time and energy to earning a living. Ironically, the stress of child-rearing is one reason why we are so quick to capitulate to our children's demands for digital entertainment. In many cases, smartphones have become our babysitters.

Traditional cultures also venerate their elders. People do not become *economically irrelevant* after a certain age. Instead they are regarded as assets, as sources of wisdom, and as repositories of cultural memory. They are never cared for by strangers or left to languish in institutions waiting to die.

Cosmologies serve to answer the deep metaphysical questions:

- Where are we from?
- Why are we here?
- Where are we going?

A shared cosmology is also a shared set of values. Traditional peoples engage in rituals and practices that serve to strengthen and affirm the bonds of the community. These practices bring a degree of social cohesion and shared meaning that is conspicuously absent in our society. We are distinctive in that we prize the individual at the expense of the community. Robert Sardello makes the observation that psychology only becomes necessary in the absence of a shared cosmology; that certain kinds of pathologies only occur in societies that force the individual to make meaning for himself rather than inherit it from the community that birthed him.

Cosmologies also give us a sense of direction, an ultimate meaning or telos toward which to orient our lives. This meaning is invariably spiritual; we are meant to serve and commune with the Creator, the Spirits, and the dead. Life has a spiritual purpose. Human beings are players in a grand cosmic drama. Although many Americans espouse spiritual values, our society is overwhelmingly materialistic. Wealth is the ultimate criterion of success. For many Americans, there is nothing beyond work, money, and spending. They imagine human beings to be little more than skin encapsulated egos destined for oblivion.

Traditional cultures also venerate the Earth. She is seen as the Mother, the source of all healing and nourishment. Plants and animals are our brethren and not merely resources to be exploited. Everything is ensouled and pulsing with spirit. Addiction is almost unknown among peoples who live in *complex resonance* with the Earth. This is not to say that those cultures are *sober* in the strict sense. Many of them use powerful psychoactive substances for religious or healing purposes. However, these plants are considered to be medicines or *spirit guides*. It would never occur to anyone to use them for purely entertainment purposes.

We can now begin to appreciate just how radically Dislocation Theory deepens and reorients our understanding of addiction. Combating addiction demands that we first understand the social and economic forces that fracture our communities. We can now amend our model of addiction to read:

RID = Dislocation

Recovery = Integration

Most alcoholics and addicts would readily agree that they suffered with RID (restless, irritable, and discontent) long before they took their first drink. This is because they were born into a largely dislocated world. The power of Dislocation Theory lies in its ability to explain both the etiology of addiction and the relative efficacy of the 12 Steps. Recovery is integrative. The steps foster integration by forging connections between the addict and God (or *higher power*), neighbor, family, and newcomer alike. Connection is the antidote to dislocation.

Unfortunately, addicts must still live and work in an overwhelmingly dislocated society. We let our kids have their iPads in the car to keep them quiet. We take it for granted that our teenagers need to stay in touch through text and Snapchat, even in the classroom, their bedroom, the car, or at the dinner table. We accept that dad and mom need to return that e-mail or text from their boss, co-worker, client, or business partner, no matter what the time or what activity the family is engaged in. We spend more time at concerts and sporting events taking selfies and shooting Instagram stories than we do listening to the music or watching the spectacle in front of us. Rather than live life we try to capture the moment and share it on social media, making sure that we use the right filter and hashtag, in order to get the brand just right. This is our *Brave New World*. Our very identities are *networked* and/or *branded*. At the same time, we have lost the capacity to be alone. We no longer appreciate the value and benefits of solitude. We can no longer be alone with ourselves, even as we have become increasingly lonely.

We sense that something is very wrong and getting worse. Yet we find it difficult to speak about it. We realize that it will not be solved by merely pointing fingers. We know that our best thinking brought us here. Addiction, wealth disparity, and ecological disaster are bearing down on us. Can we face this reality? Or will we continue along the path of least resistance and give ourselves over to any one of the myriad diversions at our fingertips. Because in the last analysis we have to make a choice—either face the truth of what we've become or spend all of our time and energy trying to evade it. We may not be able to fix every problem we look at, but we will never fix a problem that we ignore.

Once more, we cannot begin to understand dislocation outside of the context of globalization. We are at the mercy of economic forces that are either indifferent or hostile to human and ecological well-being. Economic interest trumps all. We have taken the advice of the IMF and World Bank and have privatized, cut taxes for the wealthy, and slashed social spending. These policies have only served the rich; most Americans are treading water or sinking. Communities are increasingly dislocated. Addiction follows in the wake of social fragmentation. We must face the fact that addiction is a pandemic that even the most spiritually powerful treatment modalities can barely ameliorate, that our lives are at the mercy of forces that we have only begun to understand. We cannot treat or incarcerate our way out of this problem. Nor should we hope for a quick fix. We agree with Alexander who maintains that the solution to a problem of this magnitude is a matter of *epochal social change*. Ours is a grassroots movement that understands that it is working for the sake of future generations. At its core is a tribe of activists who wed 12-Step Spirituality to Dislocation Theory.

INDIVIDUAL SELFISHNESS VERSUS SOCIETAL SIN

Because Bill Wilson wanted to distance AA from its Christian (and specifically Oxford Group) origins, he never used the term *sin* in the *Big Book*. Instead, he asserted that alcoholism is caused by *selfishness*. Despite the change in terminology, the *Big Book* sits squarely within the orthodox Christian tradition. Bill's notion of selfishness is virtually synonymous with the Augustinian notion of sin. Augustine would have understood addiction to be rooted in *concupiscence* or *disordered desire*. The addict sins because he seeks fulfillment from something other than God. Given that, the reader may note a certain tension between the *Big Book's* identification of selfishness as the root cause of alcoholism and Alexander's thesis that the etiology of addiction is ultimately social.

It is important that we reconcile this apparent contradiction because, if we don't, 12-steppers will remain stuck in the *individual pathology* camp. The *Big Book* is distinctive in that it insists that the solution is ultimately spiritual. However, its notion of selfishness blinds it to the larger societal context of addiction. If one really believes that addiction is a matter of individual selfishness, then social conditions are of little import. Fortunately, we can resolve this conundrum by appealing to the thought of Ignacio Martin-Baro.

Martin-Baro (1942–1989) was a psychologist and Jesuit priest who was murdered by a U.S.-trained death squad in El Salvador. He was also the founder of *Liberation Psychology*. Although his work has exerted a profound influence upon many thinkers (most notably Bruce Alexander), he is almost unknown in the United States. Martin-Baro argues that the notion of individual sin must be complemented with an understanding of what he calls *societal sin*. Societal sin refers to those structures or institutions that promote or reward the worst inclinations of human nature, namely avarice, competition, and violence—the same forces that destroy communities and cause dislocation.

We believe that Martin-Baro's concept of societal sin serves as a much-needed corrective to the insularity of the 12-Step world. Most 12-steppers labor in a small arena. While the *Big Book* stresses that the recovered alcoholic must work to help his fellows, its focus is almost exclusively confined to the individual alcoholic and his small circle of family and friends. 12-steppers do little or nothing to address addiction from a macro perspective. This is why we are so adamant about activism. We can no longer remain silent about the forces driving addiction and hampering recovery. But we must remain mindful that dislocation affects everyone! Addiction is only one of its more visible symptoms. Dislocation Theory can help us find common cause with large segments of the population, with addicts and non-addicts alike. Such is its power.

Martin-Baro's critique of the mental health system is of special interest to us. Psychologist and author Bruce Levine writes that Martin-Baro had argued that the "U.S. corporatocracy uses mental health professionals to manipulate and medicate people to adjust and thereby maintain the status quo."[2] We agree with this analysis. Addicts are not defective individuals, they are simply trying to adapt to life in a sick society. Our symptoms tell us as much about the world around us as they do ourselves. But the social context of addiction is almost never addressed by politicians, professors, or the media. Our elected officials will only debate the relative merits of treatment versus punishment. Martin-Baro argues that we must challenge the status quo—the powers that be—if we are to effect healing on a societal level. This means we must provide the recovery community with the information that reveals how and why people became addicts in the first place—information that makes the connection between addiction, globalization, Big Pharma, and the prison-industrial complex. In other words, we need to look at addiction through the lens of societal sin. Which institutions are at fault? And who profits from this catastrophe? We will begin with an analysis of the pivotal role played by Big Pharma.

NOTES

1. https://www.npr.org/sections/health-shots/2012/01/02/144431794/what-vietnam-taught-us-about-breaking-bad-habits. Full study is at https://onlinelibrary.wiley.com/doi/abs/10.1111/j.1521-0391.2010.00046.x.
2. http://www.truth-out.org/opinion/item/27244-why-an-assassinated-psychologist-ignored-by-us-psychologists-is-being-honored (Bruce E. Levine, "Why an Assassinated Psychologist—Ignored by U.S. Psychologists—Is Being Honored," Truthout, November 2014, accessed February 13, 2016).

10

BIG PHARMA

(Disclaimer: this is not an anti-medication book. We support harm reduction and the judicious use of medication. However, we are concerned that the reader understand how Big Pharma promotes false narratives that have harmed consumers and helped perpetuate the opioid epidemic.)

The pharmaceutical industry, with its promise of chemical cures, is a major stakeholder in the recovery industry. The medicalization of addiction—its designation as a mental illness—puts treatment under the purview of psychiatry. The medical profession, however, has made little headway in treating addiction. This holds true for other mental disorders as well. Big Pharma has done little to ameliorate conditions like depression, despite having spent billions of dollars in research and development. More and more people are medicated even as mental illness disability rates soar. One would assume that if these pharmaceutical interventions really worked, Supplemental Security Income (SSI) and Social Security Disability Insurance (SSDI) enrollment would fall.

We were stunned to learn that the *chemical imbalance* theory of mental illness was a weak hypothesis at best. Like many addicts, our providers had insisted that our abuse of drugs and alcohol was a misguided and unconscious attempt to *medicate* some underlying and undiagnosed mental disorder. We were told that we would only achieve lasting sobriety if we treated the underlying chemical imbalance as well.

Remarkably, lack of evidence for the chemical imbalance theory has long been acknowledged by many of the most prominent members of the academic and medical establishments. U.S. Surgeon General, David Satcher, in his 1999 report on mental health, wrote that "the precise causes of mental disorders are not known."[1] In 2005, Kenneth Kendler, co-editor-in-chief of *Psychological Medicine*, wrote, "We have hunted for big, simple neurochemical explanations for psychiatric disorders and we have not found them."[2] This information, however, never made its way into public awareness. By some accounts, 80% of Americans still believe that mental disorders are caused by chemical imbalances.

In 1980, the American Psychiatric Association (APA) amended its regulatory practices to allow it to receive financing from the pharmaceutical industry. This clear conflict of interest went unchallenged. Psychiatric medications are now the first line of defense in the treatment of mental disorders. Massive advertising campaigns have conditioned the American public to believe that human suffering is essentially a function of biology. The result: pills are more and more frequently prescribed as a first, and too often only, option.

THE MEDICALIZATION OF HUMAN SUFFERING

From 1974 to 1996 alcoholism and drug addiction were disability eligible conditions. In 1996 the Clinton administration abruptly ended this policy. However, this change did not result in a shrinkage of the disability rolls. Most addicts kept their benefits by getting a secondary mental health diagnosis (e.g., anxiety, depression, ADHD). The change in policy effectively incentivized mental illness for many addicts. They needed a mental health diagnosis to retain their benefits. This marked the advent of dual diagnosis (i.e., addiction and mental illness). What is routinely touted as *cutting-edge* substance abuse treatment is less a product of research than a creature of disability reform.

A New York University professor, Dr. Helena Hansen, writes: "Qualifying and recertifying for Social Security payments on the basis of psychiatric disability requires clinical assessments and medical records that demonstrate functional impairment from mental illness. Social Security applicants are advised to stay on high-dose anti-psychotics and mood stabilizers as evidence of severe, disabling symptoms, despite their side effects, in order to strengthen their case for disability benefits. As a result, maintenance medications (such as anti-psychotics and mood stabilizers combined with methadone) and Social Security payments based on co-occurring psychiatric disorders enable low-income, opioid-addicted people to survive, but also marginalize them socially and economically."[3]

This policy created a perverse financial motive to diagnose, or be diagnosed, as mentally ill. Economically challenged addicts and alcoholics needed a psychiatric diagnosis to keep their benefits. Big Pharma saw massive market growth and increased revenue as hundreds of thousands of addicts and alcoholics applied for SSDI. Billions of taxpayer dollars now flow to Big Pharma via the community mental health system. Mental health disability is now one of the main economic engines of the pharmaceutical industry—and everyone involved in the system knows it.

This also explains why graduate programs in counseling and social work pay scant attention to the role played by social factors (e.g., poverty, racism, and intergenerational trauma) in the etiology of addiction. There is simply no money in it. But promoting the idea that addiction and *mental illness* are essentially biological conditions (and therefore amenable to pharmacological treatment) is extremely lucrative. The system is designed to serve the interests of Big Pharma and the psychiatric profession (with counselors and social workers largely serving as obedient minions).

It should be emphasized that psychiatric *treatment* in itself is a major (and underreported) cause of addiction. ADD and ADHD are almost always treated with stimulant medications like Ritalin, Adderall, or Concerta—which are highly addictive drugs. In years past we were told that stimulants had a *paradoxical effect*—that they actually *slowed* down those suffering from what was then called *hyperactivity disorder*. This is not true. Stimulants affect everyone the same way. They mimic the actions of adrenaline and dopamine, which enhance the ability to focus—the main reason why stimulants are so popular with college students. Stimulants also dampen the emotions, rendering them *shallow*. Even the psychiatric establishment acknowledges the failure of these drugs to improve ADHD behaviors over the long term. The 1994 edition of the APA Textbook of Psychiatry states: "Stimulants do not produce lasting improvements in aggressivity, conduct disorder, education achievement, job functioning, marital relationships, or long-term adjustment."[4] Needless to say, this information is rarely disseminated through the media. Rates of stimulant abuse have skyrocketed in recent years. We are currently in the midst of an Adderall epidemic which receives little attention because of the magnitude of the opioid crisis.

Anxiety and panic disorders are almost universally treated with benzodiazepines (*benzos*). This class of medications include Xanax, Valium, Klonopin, and Ativan. These are highly addictive and dangerous drugs, and when mixed with alcohol (as is often the case) can lead to overdoses or even death. Unsupervised withdrawal from these drugs can even be lethal. Yet we see scores of clients who report that they were prescribed these drugs even after they told their providers that they were active alcoholics. Presumably, their doctors believed that the benzo would *treat* the underlying anxiety, freeing the patient from the need to self-medicate with alcohol. We have never seen that happen. Instead, the alcoholic almost always abuses both alcohol and benzo together. This is a recipe for disaster since this combination usually results in blackout.

However, the addiction epidemic got exponentially worse after we changed our approach to the treatment of pain. The current opioid crisis exploded in 1996 after the Veterans Administration designated pain as the fifth vital sign. (JCAHO, the Joint Commission for the Accreditation of Healthcare Organizations, made it a standard in 2001.) This was a controversial move as pain (unlike temperature, blood pressure, respiration, and pulse) cannot be objectively measured. Healthcare organizations can now be penalized if they do not ask their patients about their *level* of pain (a scale of 1 to 10). Adoption of this policy led to an almost immediate spike in pharmaceutical opioid addiction. The medical establishment, however, denied that there was an issue by insisting that untreated pain was a major medical problem in the United States. They even suggested that their critics suffered from "opiophobia."

PSEUDOADDICTION AND OTHER TALL TALES

During this same period, doctors were being taught that it was safe to increase dosages for pain management patients as the pain effectively neutralized the euphoria produced by the drug. A similar rationale lay behind the widely promoted concept of *pseudoaddiction*. Someone suffering from pseudoaddiction will have an identical symptomatology to someone who is actually addicted. Both present with the following profile:

- Isolation
- Hopelessness
- Anxiety
- Mood instability
- Fear or panic
- Anger or frustration
- Nervousness or irritability
- Low energy
- Insomnia
- Relationship issues
- Withdrawal from social activities
- Loss of interest in hobbies and leisure activities

How then do we make the distinction between true addiction and pseudo-addiction? The claim is that although pseudoaddiction looks exactly like opiate addiction, it is actually *caused by the under-prescription of pain medication*. Pain management patients are not seeking drugs because they are addicted, but because their pain has not been properly treated (i.e., the dosage is too low). For over 20 years this convoluted logic has been used to justify prescribing ever larger dosages to those who are already physically dependent. It makes no sense. If I deliberately place my hand on a hot stove, I will suffer a burn. If I accidentally put my hand on a hot stove, I still suffer a burn. My intent does not change the outcome.

But it gets even more bizarre. Big Pharma justified their marketing by repeatedly citing a one paragraph letter written in 1980 by Dr. Hershel Jick and Jane Porter. The letter, published in the *New England Journal of*

Medicine, was titled *Addiction Rare in Patients Treated with Narcotics.* It detailed an analysis of 12,000 hospitalized patients who received at least one dose of narcotics. It reported that only four patients became drug dependent. That a one paragraph letter (now known as Porter and Jick) could be used to justify a vast change in the treatment of pain is mind-boggling. None of the companies that used it bothered to do basic due diligence. They simply took it for granted that it was a peer reviewed study. It was not. And no one took note of the fact that the patients in the study were only briefly hospitalized and that Jick and Porter never addressed the risk of addiction in patients who took opioids for weeks or months.

No corporation took greater advantage of the changes at JCAHO than Purdue Pharma. In 1996 they released OxyContin, claiming it was an ideal "non-addictive" painkiller for patients suffering from chronic pain. The release of OxyContin marked the beginning of the opioid epidemic, a deadly man-made tragedy that has decimated a generation and laid waste to entire communities over the last 20+ years. Purdue Pharma's marketing campaign was highly effective; downplaying OxyContin's potential for addiction led to its being used to treat many types of pain that had hitherto never been treated with opioids. From the outset Purdue hosted pain management trainings for medical professionals at luxury resorts. They also hired 671 drug reps to promote the virtues of OxyContin to primary care providers. Their marketing strategy was wildly successful. Prescriptions for opioids increased tenfold from 1996 to 2004. Sales of OxyContin would reach $1 billion by 2001, outselling Viagra.

Of course, there was nothing non-addictive about OxyContin at all. It was actually a pharmaceutical-grade heroin. And Purdue Pharma knew it all along. Demand only increased as more and more people became addicted. It was not long before reports of unscrupulous pill mills and pain clinics started appearing on TV and in the newspapers.

PILL MILLS

The pill mills of South Florida were especially notorious (Palm Beach and Broward counties were ground zero). They fed the habits of addicts from Florida to Massachusetts. Drug dealers up and down the East Coast traveled there to score bags and bags of pills to sell to hopeless addicts in their hometowns in a lucrative black market cash grab that had not been seen since the early days of crack.

Many pill mills worked on a cash-only basis, others took Medicaid. Most did not even physically examine their patients. All a client needed was an X-ray, an MRI, or a doctor's note to establish medical need. The parking lots of these clinics were almost always full of cars with license plates from Ohio, West Virginia, Kentucky, and beyond. In Broward County there was no legal mechanism by which to audit the number of pills being sold. The ride to Florida became known as the *OxyContin Express*. Addicts would carpool to Florida, get multiple scripts filled by multiple providers, and then return home with hundreds of pills to flood their local communities. The trade was especially profitable for those clients who were on SSI or SSDI. Sam Quinones, in his book *Dreamland*, reported that someone on disability could fill a script with a $3 copay and then resell the pills for as much as $10,000 on the street.

It should also be noted that many pill mills set up shop in parts of the country that had been economically devastated by the offshoring of jobs that followed in the wake of NAFTA. For example, between 2007 and 2012, 780 million hydrocodone and oxycodone pills were delivered to West Virginia, a state with a population of 1.8 million. This means that distributors deliberately targeted areas that have been aptly described as "communities of despair." These were places that would be easily seduced by drugs that provided temporary relief from all pain, whether it is physical or emotional.

Opioid sales tripled in the United States between 2000 and 2011. Sales eventually slowed, in part, because of the negative publicity and public outcry surrounding the pill mills. However, by 2011 we began to notice a bit of an uptick in heroin use. Heroin hit the streets just as it was becoming harder for addicts to obtain pharmaceutical opioids. Addicts were quick to switch over. They quickly realized that heroin is cheaper and stronger, and that it provides a bigger bang for your buck when injected intravenously. And it was easier to get since law enforcement and government agencies began cracking down on OxyContin.

The rising demand for heroin was met, in part, by a massive increase in opium production in Mexico and Afghanistan. The following table (courtesy of the White House) details the dramatic surge in opium production in Afghanistan. It also correlates those increases to per capita rates of addiction and overdose death in the United States. In 2001 there were an estimated 189,000 heroin addicts in the United States, by 2014 that number stood at 2.5 million.

We can now see that the opioid crisis is essentially *iatrogenic*—that it was actually caused by medical treatment. Big Pharma set it all in motion with deliberately deceptive marketing. This resulted in widespread addiction which, in turn, fueled an ever-increasing demand for opioids. Now, that demand is being met with heroin and the even more sinister drug

Year	Number of Hectares of Afghan Opium Grown	Number of U.S. Heroin Addicts	Number of U.S. Heroin Deaths
2001	7,600	189,000	1,779
2002	74,000	300,000	2,089
2003	80,000	400,000	2,080
2004	131,000	500,000	1,878
2005	104,000	600,000	2,009
2006	165,000	750,000	2,088
2007	193,000	900,000	2,399
2008	157,000	1,000,000	3,041
2009	123,000	1,250,000	3,278
2010	123,000	1,500,000	3,036
2011	131,000	1,750,000	4,397
2012	154,000	2,000,000	5,925
2013	209,000	2,250,000	8,260
2014	224,000	2,500,000	10,574

fentanyl. The actions of Purdue Pharma seem to be every bit as criminal as any cartel operating in Mexico or Columbia. As of this writing, Purdue Pharma and its owner, the Sackler family, have been sued by numerous states for flooding the market with highly addictive painkillers. Other states, including New York and Connecticut, are considering criminal charges. "This is essentially a crime family . . . drug dealers in nice suits and dresses," said Paul Hanly, a New York City lawyer who is a lead attorney in a huge civil action case that is playing out in federal court in Ohio and New York involving opioid manufacturers and distributors.[5]

In 2019, more than 500 U.S. cities and counties filed a class action suit accusing the Sackler family of racketeering that was connected to the family's efforts to flood the market with OxyContin.

"This nation is facing an unprecedented opioid addiction epidemic that was initiated and perpetuated by the Sackler defendants for their own financial gain," lawyers for local governments said in a complaint filed in Manhattan federal court.

For their part, the Sackler family released a statement which read, in part: "These baseless allegations place blame where it does not belong for a complex public health crisis, and we deny them." The statement further noted that OxyContin sales "represented a tiny portion of the opioid market."[6]

The suit further claims that members of the Sackler family encouraged Purdue Pharma employees to *dupe* doctors into believing that OxyContin was not addictive and could lead to an *enhanced lifestyle*.

The Sacklers "knew about the dangers of prescription opioids and pushed to increase sales despite the devastating consequences of the public health crisis," attorneys for the local governments said in the suit.

In federal court in Boston in 2019, several executives for Insys Therapeutics went on trial for racketeering for allegedly bribing doctors to push Subsys—a fentanyl painkiller—into the market. Seven executives were indicted, including a top sales executive who testified that the company paid millions of dollars in bribes to doctors across the country. The case marked the first federal criminal trial for pharmaceutical executives since the opioid crisis began. A doctor accused in the scheme was sentenced to 32 months in prison for writing fraudulent prescriptions.

The Boston trial also provided some insight into how pharmaceutical companies use big data to their advantage—specifically, to get prescription drugs into the market. Insys, executives testified, bought daily federal data that showed prescriptions and opioid purchases across the country. The firm purchased information from the Transmucosal Immediate Release Fentanyl (TIRF) Risk Evaluation and Mitigation Strategy (REMS) program, commonly known as TIRF REMS. The system is used to alert medical professionals to misuse, abuse, and addiction to fentanyl. But in this case, authorities alleged that it was used to track purchases in order to target consumers and markets.[7]

Subsys was approved solely for cancer patients with *breakthrough* pain, but Insys sold it to doctors as a painkiller for everything from back pain to arthritis to depression. The company used many dubious methods to entice doctors to prescribe, or over-prescribe, their drug, including funneling phony speaker's fees to physicians and manipulating insurance agents. In one case, the company hired a stripper to give lap dances to a doctor to entice him to write more scripts, according to trial testimony.

Company executives also made a promotional rap video set to a beat by A$AP Rocky that bragged about how the company increased sales through titration—a tactic where doctors rapidly increase dosage. Sales reps were also given bonuses for persuading doctors to increase patients' doses.

This case, along with others that are emerging both civilly and criminally, highlights the need for opiate addicts to be informed of the machinations of Big Pharma. They need to understand how the present crisis is largely manufactured and that the same industry that claims to have a solution actually had a big hand in creating the problem. Addicts need to understand that they have been manipulated, lied to, and cheated. The game—in which they are a pawn—was rigged from the start.

We must educate our loved ones about the true causes of the present catastrophe. We must also ask how we have come to be a *medicated society*. We must challenge and reject the American assumption that for every problem there is a "magic pill." Our movement is about empowering people and not simply following the lead of your doctor or co-worker. Be skeptical of slick marketing. If it sounds too good to be true, it probably is. Do your own homework. Take stock of yourself. Look yourself in the eye and ask, "What are my safest options?"

The reality is that oftentimes, an over-the-counter analgesic will work just as well as Percocet or Vicodin. And oftentimes, meditation, exercise, dietary improvements, better sleep habits, or other self-care changes, will work far more effectively than antidepressants or an anti-anxiety medication. We are not encouraging anyone to abruptly come off their psychiatric medication, but we are urging you to do your due diligence before you start a drug regimen. We hope this chapter shows that consumers cannot afford to take anything for granted. Before we avail ourselves of professional help, we need to take a deep dive and really examine what is going on in our own lives. If you're newly unemployed, eating a lot of fast food, laying around all day, immersed in social media or other screen time—it's little wonder that you're depressed. Maybe the answer is not a pill. Maybe you need to make changes in your life.

It is time that we took a hard look at the alternative modalities that have been used for centuries in India and China. We need to explore somatic and psychotherapeutic approaches that embrace and acknowledge the superordinate value of spirituality to human well-being as well. We must challenge and reject the American assumption that for every problem there is a magic pill.

SUMMARY

Big Pharma is a multi-billion dollar industry. They have a vested interest in keeping people medicated over the long term. This is why they insist that opiate addiction is a "chronically relapsing condition." It is also why they ignore the reality of the recovered addict and the efficacy of abstinence-based treatment. We always encourage our clients to ask themselves, *Cui bono?* Who benefits? The sad truth is that addicts are worth more sick than well.

In this chapter we have detailed some of the ways that Big Pharma helped create and perpetuate the addiction epidemic. But they are certainly not the only players reaping an enormous financial windfall from human ruin. There are also those who grow rich waging the war on drugs. Since the 1970s, we have spent over a trillion dollars fighting this war. We have nothing to show for it. Drugs are cheaper, more powerful, and more plentiful than ever before. And more people are dying from overdoses than ever in our history. We have also managed to lock up more of our citizens than at any other time in our history.

NOTES

1. U.S. Department of Health and Human Services, Mental Health: A Report of the Surgeon General (1999), 3, 68, 78

2. J. Lacasse, "Serotonin and Depression: a Disconnect between the Advertisements and the Scientific Literature," PloS Medicine 2 (2005): 1211–16

3. http://somatosphere.net/2015/12/pharmaceutical-prosthesis-and-white-racial-rescue-in-the-prescription-opioid-epidemic.html (Helena Hansen, "Pharmaceutical Prosthesis and White Racial Rescue in the Prescription Opioid 'Epidemic,'" Somatosphere, December 2015, accessed October 6, 2018).

4. P. Breggin, "Psychostimulants in the treatment of children diagnosed with ADHD," International Journal of Risk & Safety in Medicine 12 (1993): 3–35.

5. https://www.theguardian.com/us-news/2018/nov/19/sackler-family-members-face-mass-litigation-criminal-investigations-over-opioids-crisis

6. https://www.bostonglobe.com/news/nation/2019/03/20/sackler-family-accused-new-suit-causing-opioid-crisis/SfDUEXZoLkxKXal4WSpzhO/story.html. "Sackler family accused in new suit of causing opioid crisis," Boston Globe. March 20, 2019.

7. "Jurors Told How Insys Chief Used Competitors' Data to Drive Own Opioid Sales," Bloomberg. March 7, 2019.

11

THE WAR ON DRUG ADDICTS

The United States imprisons a higher percentage of its citizens than any country in the world. The state and federal prison population grew from 218,466 in 1974 to 1,508,636 in 2014, a nearly 600% increase. As of this writing, 46% of U.S. inmates are serving time for drug offenses—which is, by far, the largest category. (The second highest category—weapons, explosives, and arson—stands at 18%.) We are not waging a war on drugs; we are waging a war on drug addicts.[1]

While the term "war on drugs" was first coined by President Nixon in the 1970s, it only came into general parlance in the late 1980s when President Reagan vowed to win the war once and for all. While Reagan saw the beginnings of the crack scourge, it was President George H.W. Bush who was faced with the cocaine tsunami that hit America in the late '80s. Bush more than doubled the federal drug prevention budget from $5 billion to $12 billion and sent the military into action to stop overseas production and international smuggling. Billions also went to law enforcement which, by some estimates, led to one million Americans being incarcerated every year. Bush's solution was more prisons, more jails, more courts, more prosecutors.[2]

Matters got exponentially worse during the Clinton era. Shortly after taking office, President Clinton signed a $30 billion crime bill that mandated life sentences for many three-time drug offenders. It also authorized $16 billion in police and prison grants. Clinton also supported the draconian *100 to 1* sentencing ratio for crack versus powder cocaine. The adoption of those disparate sentencing guidelines—which called for 100 times the prison sentence for crack cocaine versus a powder cocaine offense—had a devastating impact upon the black community that is still being felt today.

By 2000, African Americans were being incarcerated for drug offenses at more than 26 times the rate they had been in 1983. Statistics compiled by the U.S. Sentencing Commission show that in 2009, 79% of crack offenders were black compared to just 10% who were white. The numbers for powder cocaine were strikingly different—only 28% were black and 17% were white.[3,4]

Clinton would oversee the largest increase in the federal and state prison population in U.S. history. It was during his administration that we moved into first place with the highest incarceration rate in the world. The war on drugs fueled this growth. Today, we incarcerate our citizens at a rate of 716 per 100,000 (by comparison, the U.K. locks up 147 per 100,000).

In his book *Drug Warriors and Their Prey: From Police Power to Police State*, historian Richard L. Miller paints a truly disturbing picture of the dynamics at play in the war on drugs. Miller compares the treatment of American drug addicts to what was done to German Jews during the Nazi era. He leans heavily upon the work of noted Holocaust scholar Raul Hilberg. Hilberg detailed how the German public was only gradually and systematically conditioned to regard the Jews as subhuman. The Final Solution did not occur in a vacuum but was, instead, the result of extensive propaganda and careful preparation. Many ordinary German citizens were not only complicit in, but also directly profited from, the exploitation and eventual extermination of their fellow citizens. Hilberg argued that the Holocaust occurred through a process of five steps:

1. Identification
2. Ostracism
3. Confiscation
4. Concentration
5. Annihilation

Now, following Miller's assessments, let us relate these steps to the war on drugs.

IDENTIFICATION

The process begins with fear mongering and scapegoating. A group of people—in this case, drug addicts—are identified as the cause of a wide range of societal problems. Drug addicts spread disease, they corrupt our children, they rob and steal and assault the innocent, they waste valuable resources, and their presence in our neighborhoods drives down the value of our homes. The drug addict is identified as public enemy #1.

The label *drug addict* can also be used to provide cover and justification for racist beliefs and attitudes. We cannot make being Mexican against the law, but we can criminalize a substance (i.e., marijuana) that is strongly associated (rightly or wrongly) with that group. In the 1940's, cocaine addicts were depicted as sex crazed maniacs who were impervious to bullets. Hence, we must lock up everyone (i.e., the black men) involved in the cocaine trade.

The implicit racism of the war on drugs is an established fact. While the rates of drug abuse among African-Americans and whites are comparable, the imprisonment rate of African-Americans is six times that of whites. One third of inmates serving time in state facilities are African-American even though they represent only 12.5% of illegal drug users.[5]

OSTRACISM

We only ostracize those we fear or hate. Hence, we must teach people to fear and hate drug addicts.

America was in the grip of an opiate epidemic in the decades leading up to the passage of the Harrison Act in 1914. Roughly 1 in 200 Americans were addicted to morphine or one of its many derivatives. However, most addicts were upper-class women. Addiction was viewed and treated as a medical problem. Drug addicted patients were prescribed "medicine" by their doctors. There was little stigma associated with being an addict. It was a sad but all too common phenomena.[6]

Attitudes changed with the passage of the Harrison Act. Now it was no longer a medical issue but a matter of law enforcement. Drug addicts were criminals and needed to be treated accordingly. Over the course of the 20th century, they would be thoroughly demonized and scapegoated by politicians, the media, and Hollywood alike. The war on drugs served to inflame public perception. In 1990, Los Angeles Police Department Chief Daryl Gates declared that casual drug users "ought to be taken out and shot."[7] In 1996, Hillary Clinton warned the nation about the drug dealing *superpredators* that roamed our city streets. By the end of the 20th century, ostracism of addicts was a fait accompli.

CONFISCATION

Few Americans are aware of how forfeiture laws have impacted those charged with drug offenses. Civil asset forfeiture was rarely used prior to the war on drugs. These laws empower the government to seize cash, cars, real estate, or other property suspected of being connected to criminal activity, even if the owner is never arrested for a crime. In 80% of civil asset forfeitures, criminal charges are never even filed against property owners.

Once again, these laws are disproportionately enforced against people of color. According to an ACLU report in Philadelphia, blacks account for 71% of owners who have cash forfeited without being convicted of a crime each year.[8]

Seized assets are used by law enforcement to meet budget shortfalls. This means that we have effectively incentivized the seizure of private property by law enforcement. In August 1990, Attorney General Dick Thornburgh publicly urged law enforcement to step up their efforts in seizing private assets. He said, "Every effort must be made to increase forfeiture income during the remaining three months." The amount of money seized by the Justice Department's Asset Forfeiture Fund has steadily increased over the course of the war on drugs, going from $27 million in 1985 to $4.5 billion in 2014.[9,10,11]

These laws have been horribly abused over the last thirty years. Here is but one example. In 2017, a 50-year-old Wisconsin man named Phil Parhamovich was the subject of a routine traffic stop in Wyoming.

Parhamovich, a musician, did not have a criminal record nor was he in possession of any illegal substances. However, he did have over $90,000 (his life's savings) hidden in a speaker in his car. The police officer told him he was being stopped for making an improper lane change and not wearing his seat belt. He then interrogated Parhamovich about the contents of his vehicle. Parhamovich's nervousness provided cause for the officer to call in a canine unit. The vehicle was searched after the dog allegedly got "excited." That, in turn, led to the discovery of the cash. Parhamovich was then asked to sign a waiver that would turn the money over to the State of Wyoming for drug enforcement purposes. He was also told that he would only be let go if he signed the document. Parhamovich was so intimidated that he went ahead and signed the waiver. He later got the money back, but only after his story went public and a team of attorneys fought the state.[12] This case shows how forfeiture laws are being used to confiscate the property of ordinary Americans. The war on drugs poses a threat to all of us, addict and non-addict alike.

Civil forfeitures are but the tip of the iceberg. Addicts who have been convicted of drug-related crimes see many of their rights confiscated as well. Felons may not own firearms or sit on juries. In nine states they are not allowed to vote. They cannot live in Section 8 Housing and they will likely lose their eligibility for federal student aid.

The loss of these rights has far-reaching consequences. In some counties with African-American majorities, so many black men have felony convictions that juries are almost always predominantly composed of whites. Single mothers cannot raise their families in Section 8 Housing. Their children are, in effect, punished for their parent's convictions. The loss of these rights has resulted in the disenfranchisement of a large percentage of our fellow citizens. Today, millions of Americans have criminal records. In 2011, the National Employment Law Project put the number at 65 million. Most significantly, felony convictions are a serious obstacle when it comes to finding employment since many felons feel they have no real options outside of applying for disability or returning to a life of crime.[13]

With ostracization comes exploitation. In order to survive, many addicts are forced to sell the only commodity they have left—their bodies. Sex trafficking of women and children is the fastest growing criminal industry in the world. A study found that between 40% and 85% of all prostitutes are drug users and that 55% reported being addicted prior to their becoming prostitutes.[14]

Michelle Hannan, director of the anti-human trafficking effort at the Salvation Army in central Ohio, reports that opiate addiction is a factor is virtually all of the human trafficking cases she sees.[15]

Many poor addicts also sell their blood. The United States has long been dubbed the "OPEC of plasma." And sadly, the record number of fatal opioid overdoses has actually caused a spike in the availability of organs for transplant.

CONCENTRATION

The United States reached the stage of *concentration* long ago. Now we must ask, "Who benefits from the mass incarceration of drug addicts?"

As previously noted, the 1990s saw a huge expansion of what is now known as the *prison-industrial complex* (PIC). As of this writing, the U.S. has roughly 5% of the world's population and over 20% of its inmates.

The PIC became big business after the establishment of the first private prison company—Corrections Corporation of America (CCA)—in 1983. CCA went public in 1986 and from the outset it claimed that its penitentiaries would be much cheaper to run than government-operated facilities. It cut costs by reducing correction officer salaries (the vast majority of private prisons are not unionized) and increasing the inmate-to-guard ratio. But the real money is made through the leasing of inmate labor. The private prison industry raked in $1.8 billion in 2017.[16] That profit is made off the sweat and toil of prisoners, most of whom earn less than a dollar an hour.

Here are some of the many companies that used American inmate labor as of 2018:[17]

- Abbott Laboratories
- Autozone

- Bank of America
- Bayer
- Cargill
- Caterpillar
- Chevron
- Costco
- Eli Lilly
- GlaxoSmithKline
- International Paper
- John Deere
- Johnson & Johnson
- Koch Industries
- Mary Kay
- Merck
- Motorola
- Pfizer
- Sears
- Starbucks
- United Airlines
- UPS
- Verizon
- Wendy's

Private prisons give corporations an attractive option. They can offshore manufacturing to China or some third world country or save those costs setting up shop in a private prison in the United States. Furthermore, many private prisons have "occupancy guarantee" clauses in their contracts with the state. (Montana, New Mexico, and Oklahoma have the most private prisons.) This means the state pays for the bed whether it is occupied or not. These clauses give the state a financial incentive to keep private prisons full. It also provides a measure of insurance for the corporations who have leased inmate labor from the prison.

The PIC is a big part of the new economy. Whole industries have sprung up to service prisons, their employees, and their occupants. Prisoners need to be fed and clothed; contracts for mental health and medical services are highly lucrative. In the aftermath of NAFTA, prisons have also become the biggest employer in many rural communities. We are heavily invested in the machinery of mass incarceration.

The legal system itself has evolved so as to insure the steady flow of inmates into the prison pipeline. As of 2013, 97% of federal and 94% of state defendants pled guilty as a result of a plea bargain agreement. Plea bargains are so ubiquitous that they are, in effect, the essence of the American criminal justice system. If even 10% of cases went to trial the entire criminal justice system would grind to a halt.

Starting in the 1970s we saw wave upon wave of "tough-on-crime" legislation. Criminal codes were revised toward much tougher sentencing (e.g., mandatory minimums). These changes also criminalized many more behaviors, which has led to defendants being charged with significantly more crimes than they were 50 years ago. This, in turn, has given prosecutors enormous leverage when offering plea bargains. Judges often have little discretion in sentencing. If the prosecutor chooses to charge someone with a crime that carries a mandatory minimum sentence, the judge may be forced to sentence someone to prison for decades for a relatively minor infraction.

Changes in the criminal codes have resulted in the state regularly prosecuting people for possessing small amounts of illegal substances or for merely having drug paraphernalia. Furthermore, the far more serious charge of *intent to distribute* is highly subjective and is often determined by nothing more than police testimony. (It should be noted that we did not arrest millions of Americans for possession of alcohol during Prohibition—and in countries like Portugal and the Netherlands virtually no one is imprisoned for simple possession.)

By way of example, let's take the case of Sandra Avery. In 2005 she was arrested with 50 grams of crack cocaine and charged with possession with intent to deliver. That amount automatically brings a mandatory minimum 10-year sentence. Avery elected to take it to trial and was convicted (as are 90% of federal defendants who choose to go to trial) and sentenced to life. The prosecution was able to seek a life sentence because Avery had three prior convictions for possession. However, she only had small amounts of crack in those earlier cases—together, it amounted to a total value of less than $100.[18]

Again, our prisons are full of drug addicts, most of whom are nonviolent. The Huffington Post found that about 1.5 million people are arrested each year on drug charges—80% of those are for simple possession. That means we are arresting and incarcerating users and addicts. Contrary to the law enforcement or government party line, our resources are not generally going toward arresting violent drug dealers or taking down major kingpins; they are going toward putting addicts in jail. In the age of the plea bargain, it is all too easy for a prosecutor to convict defendants who do not present any danger to society but are in actuality suffering from addiction, poverty, or a serious mental disorder. We have not only disenfranchised millions of drug addicts, but we have also moved far down the road toward criminalizing poverty, addiction, and mental illness.[19]

Addicts are not only concentrated in jails and prisons, they are also herded, through government policies and economic and societal forces, to live in certain neighborhoods and towns. Because felons have difficulty finding housing, they tend to gravitate to poorer neighborhoods and places that are usually lacking services or employment opportunities. The economies of these areas are almost invariably dominated by the drug trade. Many of these towns and neighborhoods were once solidly middle class. However, where there were once well-paying manufacturing jobs, the only options left are at McDonald's and the Dollar Store. For many people living in these areas, dealing drugs is the only economic decision. They simply have no other options.

America loves a Horatio Alger story—but it is beginning to wear thin. We want to believe that anyone with enough drive and smarts can make it big in the United States. Unfortunately, it just isn't so for millions of people. We need to reckon with this reality if we are going to really understand the true nature of the opioid epidemic. It is as much a tale of greed, poverty, corruption, and racism as it is a story about heroin, OxyContin, and opioid use disorder.

ANNIHILATION

We imagine that most of our readers are saying, "Well, this isn't Nazi Germany. We aren't executing addicts." And strictly speaking, they are right. But it behooves us to remember that the drug trade is extremely violent and that incarcerated addicts cannot parent children. And according to the Prison Policy Initiative, every year spent in prison takes two years off a person's life expectancy. It is estimated that having over two million Americans locked up has actually shortened overall life expectancy in the United States by five years. And then there are the overdoses . . .[20]

We are continually approached by clients who tell us something like, "But what merchant kills his customer? It's just not a good business model." Fentanyl is killing so many people that our clients are beginning to wonder if it is actually deliberate. Although that sounds like the most outrageous of conspiracy theories, they are quick to point out that fentanyl is frequently showing up in batches of coke, Xanax, crystal meth, and even LSD. This means that consumers are unwittingly buying fentanyl-laced drugs, and that fentanyl is killing people who do not even abuse opiates. We cannot say if this is deliberate or part of some grand scheme to cull the population by killing drug addicts, but we do know that addicts are dying in record numbers and the only solution being promoted by our political leaders and the medical establishment is to prescribe them still more addictive drugs.[21,22,23,24]

NOTES

1. https://www.bop.gov/about/statistics/statistics_inmate_offenses.jsp
2. https://www.washingtonpost.com/outlook/2018/12/06/george-hw
   -bushs-biggest-failure-war-drugs/?utm_term=.e008ce288c2e
3. https://www.usnews.com/news/articles/2010/08/03/data-show-racial
   -disparity-in-crack-sentencing
4. https://www.thenation.com/article/hillary-clinton-does-not-deserve
   -black-peoples-votes/

5. https://www.naacp.org/criminal-justice-fact-sheet/

6. https://www.smithsonianmag.com/history/inside-story-americas
-19th-century-opiate-addiction-180967673/

7. *Los Angeles Times*, "Casual Drug Users Should Be Shot, Gates Says,"
Sept. 6, 1990

8. http://www.drugpolicy.org/issues/asset-forfeiture-reform

9. https://www.nytimes.com/1993/05/31/us/seized-property-in-crime
-cases-causes-concern.html

10. https://scholarlycommons.law.northwestern.edu/cgi/viewcontent
.cgi?article=6741&context=jclc

11. https://www.postandcourier.com/news/money-property-and-drugs
-do-controversial-civil-asset-forfeiture-laws/article_0fe3f320-3cba
-11e7-bd00-17bfbb574dc5.html

12. https://www.vox.com/policy-and-politics/2017/12/1/16686014/
phillip-parhamovich-civil-forfeiture

13. https://www.theatlantic.com/magazine/archive/2017/09/innocence
-is-irrelevant/534171/

14. http://www.orchidrecoverycenter.com/blog/sex-trafficking-america
-opioid-crisis2/

15. http://www.sideeffectspublicmedia.org/post/how-heroin-traps-women
-cycle-sex-work-and-addiction

16. https://www.foxnews.com/opinion/the-cold-hard-facts-about
-americas-private-prison-system

17. https://www.peoplesworld.org/article/corporations-and-governments
-collude-in-prison-slavery-racket/

18. https://www.forbes.com/sites/jacobsullum/2013/12/08/why-97-of
-federal-drug-offenders-plead-guilty/#20465bb15db0

19. https://www.huffingtonpost.com/entry/4-reasons-why-the-us-needs
-to-decriminalize-drugs-and-why-were-closer-than-you-think_us
_5963e1bde4b005b0fdc7926e

20. https://www.prisonpolicy.org/blog/2017/06/26/life_expectancy/

21. https://www.webmd.com/mental-health/addiction/news/20181031/
fentanyl-laced-crack-cocaine-a-deadly-new-threat#1

22. https://www.cbsnews.com/news/fake-xanax-can-be-a-killer/

23. https://montreal.ctvnews.ca/dangerous-drug-carfentanyl-found-on
-blotting-papers-in-laval-1.3801420

24. https://www.courier-journal.com/story/news/crime/2018/05/03/
meth-resurgence-drug-epidemic-fentanyl/447191002/

12

PERILS AND PITFALLS

Given all that we have discussed, it would seem that the deck is stacked against addicts—that the game is rigged. Make no mistake—it is. Still, there is hope. Here are five common outcomes for the addict attempting recovery:

1. Recovered
2. Recovery—relapse(s)—recovered
3. Abstinence or *white knuckling*
4. Chronic relapse
5. Permanent relapse—death

The first outcome is relatively rare but numerically significant. One is "recovered" as a result of the *psychic change* brought about by following the 12 Steps or through some other spiritual means. We do not believe that this can only occur via the 12 Steps, but it is the best method we have found. Many addicts have found—and continue to find—permanent recovery through religion and/or other means.

The second outcome is essentially the same as the first, the only difference being that the addict relapses one or more times in the process of following the steps before he or she finally *gets it*. The third outcome is all too common. Many addicts and alcoholics achieve lasting sobriety, but are bedeviled by the feelings of RID (restless, irritable, and discontent) and mental obsession.

The fourth group—chronic relapsers—are the largest, sadly. Chronic relapsers are the cash cow of the industry. They are in and out of treatment, on and off medication, in and out of psychotherapy. Some stay on medication-assisted treatment (MAT) for the long term, others come off it. We hope that our readers can see that the claim that opiate addiction is a "chronically relapsing" condition only profits those who make that claim. Relapse is not inevitable, although it does happen frequently. This is why we are adamant that our voices be heard. Recovered opiate addicts are a reality. They are not on MAT and, at the same time, they have demonstrated that they know how to help their fellow addicts *get recovered* as well. The media does opiate addicts and their loved ones a great disservice by continually repeating the lie that "abstinence kills." They are promoting the idea that recovery is impossible.

The last group—permanent relapsers—is hardest to quantify because they quickly vanish and aren't heard from again. Most die. Too many. The mortality rate of addicts has been rising steadily for years.

Some AA members claim that Bill Wilson said that the only sentence that he would change in the *Big Book* was the one that reads, "Rarely have we seen a person fail who has thoroughly followed our path" (*Big Book* p. 58). Supposedly, Bill would have replaced *rarely* with *never*. While we do not know if this anecdote is true, we agree with the sentiment. The problem, however, is that many addicts do not finish the process—or if they do, they fail to grow beyond the twelfth step.

To truly surrender, those addicts must come to the realization that they cannot fix themselves or *think through* the drink. They must surrender the whole of themselves, and not just their addictions. Recovery is largely a function of the depth of their surrender. Later, they will experience a degree of relief beyond what they thought possible. But it all begins with an act of surrender. In time, they will come to understand that they have been redeemed—that they surrendered their old selves for the sake of something greater. They will be energized to share the good news with those still suffering with active addiction.

Sadly, while social media has made it easier than ever to contact someone, it is much harder to reach (emotionally, intellectually, and spiritually) addicts than it was 20 years ago. For many newcomers, a pure 12-Step approach no longer suffices. The addiction epidemic is so massive and complex that we need to reconsider our approach. (This is one of the main reasons why we are such strong proponents of yoga and Dislocation Theory.) We are seeing more hopelessness, apathy, and despair. It is getting harder and harder to get traction with clients, especially millennial males. Some of this has to do with the very nature of opioid addiction, but other factors include chronic stress and the aforementioned perils of the digital age. In this chapter, we will discuss how we can best meet these challenges.

Because opiates have been getting stronger and cheaper, the severity of addiction has been getting exponentially worse. Withdrawal is that much more strenuous in the age of fentanyl. In opiate addiction, the brain mistakes narcotics for endorphins. Because it is designed to maintain a state of homeostasis, the body responds to what it takes to be a surplus of endorphins by shutting down endorphin production. Endorphins serve a multitude of functions, including the regulation of mood, sleep, and pain. They are naturally produced during sex, breastfeeding, exercise, or when we share the company of those we love and trust. Heroin produces a blissful, pain-free euphoria. When the addict gets high, their brain is awash in *artificial endorphins*.

Unfortunately, when they detox, the pendulum swings violently in the other direction. They go into a state of *endorphin deficit*. Opiate withdrawal is an agonizing protracted experience. For many addicts the insomnia and pain are the least of it. The real torture is the racing mind and unrelenting emotional duress. These symptoms are what make opiate withdrawal so challenging. They are also a major reason why so many addicts stay on methadone and/or suboxone for years, or even lifetimes; it's a relief from the pain.

The good news is that Mother Nature will heal the brain in due time. We emphatically reject the argument that people who report "feeling better" on narcotics suffer from some inherent endorphin deficiency. This is just another argument designed to sell MAT. Emotions are contextual—they provide valuable data about what is going on in our lives and within our psyches. If we take medications to blunt their affect, then we cannot hear the messages coming from within. Emotional distress tells us that something is wrong. It also points the way forward. RID actually informs us of what needs to be addressed if we are to heal. This is the work of 12-Step recovery. We cannot address that constellation of emotions if we are over-medicated or getting high. This is why many clinicians will not work with clients who are in active addiction. (It is also one of the reasons why we insist that MAT is not treatment.) When we are using, we cannot face, feel, or name the demons that are driving our addiction. Likewise, if we suppress or patholo-gize our symptoms (e.g., depression or anxiety), then we will never be able to get down to the root causes of our condition. It stands to reason that an addict with five warrants out for his or her arrest might be anxious, or that an alcoholic who is facing imminent divorce would be depressed. These are normal reactions to extreme circumstances. Too often, a dual diagnosis misinterprets effect for cause, meaning it is quick to conclude that anxiety is the cause of the addiction and not its effect.

We also do not believe that addicts need to be entirely free of with-drawal symptoms before they commence taking steps. Feeling raw and vulnerable is a powerful impetus for recovery. And if you do not give newly sober addicts something productive to do, they will drive them-selves crazy fixating on their withdrawal symptoms. To be part of a com-munity of men and women who are writing inventory and practicing meditation while in the throes of withdrawal is a powerful experience in and of itself. They are demonstrating to themselves and one another that they can fight the dragon of addiction—that they are more than capable of meeting the challenge confronting them. This can only happen when working steps in a communal setting.

There are a few simple but very effective actions that the addict can do to support the healing of the brain. They are:

- Meditation and/or contemplation
- Concentration
- Novel activity
- Aerobic exercise
- Diet

HEALING THE BRAIN

The benefits of meditation and/or contemplation for recovering addicts and alcoholics cannot be overstated. Physically, meditation has been shown to lower blood pressure, decrease stress-related pain, and increase serotonin production. Psychologically, meditation decreases anxiety and improves focus and peace of mind. It is enormously enhanced when done in conjunction with yoga or tai chi.

We practice concentration when we engage in strenuous mental activity. This could be reading or playing chess or doing Sudoku or crossword puzzles. These activities serve to discipline the attention; they still the racing mind and create new neural pathways in the brain.

Novelty also creates new pathways in the brain. Happily, novelty is *built-in* to recovery. Everything is new—sobriety itself, the fellowship, the awakening to genuine feeling. It is imperative that addicts not fall into old patterns of behavior. This, in itself, is a strong argument for extended care and/or sober living. We recommend that addicts avoid returning home if at all feasible. It is important that they break old patterns of behavior and use the tools they have just acquired to meet the challenges ahead. Too often, addicts return home to families who try to shield them from the stresses of daily life. These stresses, however, are the *raw material* of recovery; addicts cannot recover if they do not learn how to deal with life without drugs or alcohol. Recovery is all about change—it should be encouraged and embraced.

The value of aerobic exercise is obvious. It helps to oxygenate the blood and to jump start endorphin production. Vigorous exercise also goes a long way toward improving one's sense of well-being and self-esteem.

Addicts and alcoholics are notorious for eating junk food or not eating at all. In early recovery, one should try to avoid the usual culprits (e.g., aspartame, high fructose corn syrup, hydrogenated and partially hydrogenated oils, white sugar, fried foods) as much as possible. A sound diet will include plenty of grains, fruits, and vegetables; a moderate amount of protein; and plenty of good fats (e.g., fish, flaxseed oil, olive oil). A healthy diet will help the addict in virtually every domain of life—from sleeping to concentration to self-esteem.

Please note that all of the aforementioned actions are non-pharmacological and are either free or relatively cheap.

DIGITAL ADDICTION

The digital age has brought with it an array of challenges that were unimaginable a short 25 years ago. Clients today often present with an array of symptoms that were once quite rare. These include a shortened attention span, issues of identity, and a generalized apathy. It is markedly worse in our younger male clients, who appear to be suffering what might be described as a *loss of social intelligence.*

The plight of young American men has caught the attention of several researchers, most notably Dr. Philip Zimbardo. Zimbardo, who is emeritus professor of psychology at Stanford, first noticed these changes in his male students several years ago. His observations led him to research the phenomena; he relates his findings in the book, *Man, Interrupted.*

Millennial men are falling behind their female counterparts in almost every measurable category. Young men are less educated and more likely to be unemployed. Women are also finally beginning to close the income gap throughout the developed world—which is a good thing. Zimbardo believes that the *failure to thrive* we see in many young men is largely due to several factors, including:

1. Digital gaming
2. Digital pornography
3. Stimulant medication
4. Diminished economic prospects

Gaming is an extremely popular and overwhelmingly male activity. It is not uncommon for young men to play for six, eight, or even 10 hours or more at a stretch. Gaming addiction is a very real and increasingly problematic phenomena. Gaming stimulates the production of dopamine. It activates the same neural pathways that are affected by cocaine, stimulants, or crystal meth.

Digital games often employ avatars, which allow players to assume personas that are very different from their real identity. Being an almost exclusively male pastime, gaming reinforces and encourages a certain kind of interaction that has little social value outside the gamer world. Self-esteem is largely a function of how well the gamer performs and of how well regarded his skills are held by the other players. It is a hermetically sealed world; hard core gaming does not help young men develop the kind of social skills needed in a job interview or when asking someone out on a date.

As dangerous as gaming addiction is, it pales in comparison to digital pornography. Where alcoholism progresses by volume (the amount of alcohol consumed), porn addiction progresses by novelty. This means that the addict's taste in pornography grows increasingly bizarre and extreme as the addiction progresses. Unfortunately, all manner of pornographic material is readily available in the digital age. Most boys today have been exposed to images that would have been unavailable (and sometimes unimaginable) just a few short years ago. And most young men become consumers of digital pornography long before they become sexually active.

The consequences of digital porn addiction are startling. Rates of sexual dysfunction in young men have skyrocketed. Many report that they are not aroused by conventional sexual behavior. This is all the more striking given that millennials are actually having less sex than previous generations. Men are also reporting problems interacting with women. They complain of shyness and an inability to initiate conversation. Digital pornography is driving a huge wedge in between the sexes.

Most stimulant medication (e.g., Adderall, Ritalin, Concerta) is prescribed to men between the ages of 18 and 25, leading some to dub this group *Generation Adderall.* A Harvard study (Zimbardo 2016) demonstrated that lab animals that had been exposed to stimulant medication as juveniles showed a conspicuous lack of drive as adults. A joint study conducted by researchers from Brown, Tufts, and UCLA (Zimbardo 2016) revealed that these drugs cause damage to the nucleus accumbens (the same part of the brain implicated in addiction) in human beings. Furthermore, a small nucleus accumbens in humans correlates with low motivation or apathy. This is the most disturbing symptom that we see in many of our younger male clients. They show little initiative or interest in much of anything, especially recovery. They have difficulty making and sustaining eye contact or initiating conversation. Many of them lack muscle tone as they never played sports or performed manual labor. They don't read or take an interest in politics or culture. It really appears as if their lives have been shaped by drugs, gaming, and digital pornography.

We have already noted that millennial men also face an unprecedented degree of economic uncertainty. This has led many young men to give up, get on the disability rolls, or deal drugs. For better or worse, the image of the hardworking breadwinner has long been one of the dominant masculine archetypes of American culture. It no longer seems obtainable for many young men.

Zimbardo's research dovetails neatly with Dislocation Theory. Digital culture is having a corrosive effect on human connection, especially between the sexes. Economic stressors are further exacerbating the problem. These problems need to be discussed. There is no evidence that we will ever return to the halcyon days of post-WWII America when high school graduates could work their way into the middle class. In 21st-century America, sudden economic displacement is a fact of life. We cannot halt the furious advance of technology. Instead, we must learn how to ameliorate the effects of digital culture. Recovering heroin addicts can avoid being around heroin. We cannot adopt that same strategy with digital devices. They are embedded in everything we do. They are part of our job, our socialization, and our relationships. They are here to stay.

With the intrusion of digital devices into our lives, it is easy to see why so many of our clients lack soft skills. We have spoken with human resource professionals who tell us that it is becoming harder and harder to find prospective employees who can stand up straight, look people in the eye, and arrive at work on time. Public speaking and basic writing skills are also hard to find and are in high demand. These are still more reasons why addicts should go into extended care and/or sober living. It gives them an opportunity to learn and polish many of these soft skills. Quality sober living will provide coaching on the basics of writing a resume, preparing for an interview, and managing a paycheck. And all addicts need to learn even more basic skills like cooking, cleaning, and doing laundry. Millennial addicts have more problems in these areas than do their older peers.

We also believe that psychotherapy can be a powerful adjunct to step work. Couples counseling is especially valuable. Many relationships do not survive sobriety. This is even true in cases of genuine recovery. A good definition of an addict is: "someone who cannot do relationships." Like everything else in the addict's world, intimate relationships are mediated through drug abuse. That is, addicts use drugs to deal with the emotional challenges of being partnered. Needless to say, most of them need to learn how to communicate effectively. This takes time and patience. A recovery-savvy therapist will know how to model and facilitate effective communication. He or she will be able to counsel patience and help the couple realize that, in many significant respects, they are starting a new relationship. We have also observed that a lot of sponsors, even those who are highly experienced, are not always particularly skilled or qualified to provide direction in this area. This makes sense given that they are addicts themselves. Hence, we believe there is no shame in the sponsor referring the sponsored party to couples therapy. In many cases it is the ethical thing to do.

RECOVERY AND INITIATION

There are also many therapists who work out of an explicitly spiritual orientation. They may identify themselves as Jungian, pastoral, Buddhist, or transpersonal. Generally, their training and orientation makes them far more sympathetic and understanding of the meaning and significance of the 12-Step process. Recovering addicts sometimes find that these practitioners provide a dimension of depth that can be hard to find with a sponsor. These therapists can also be invaluable resources for the seasoned 12-steppers who are looking to expand their spiritual horizons.

Genuine recovery is essentially initiatory. The addicts must die to their old selves if they are to be reborn as *recovered addicts*. Recovered addicts become, in turn, wounded healers. They know addiction and recovery from the inside out and can usher others through what can be a very harrowing process. In traditional cultures, the vocation of healer or shaman is often preceded by a life-threatening illness. The sickness is understood to be initiatory, a descent into the realm of death. Healing is imagined as rebirth. The old identity is left behind and the initiate is reborn a healer. In traditional cultures, healers are accorded great respect. Their presence is believed to be essential to the well-being of the community.

Recovered addicts are shown no such respect. Although they serve a similar function as healer-shamans, their work goes largely unnoticed.

They occupy a liminal space where they are really only fully acknowledged by those they help. Like the shaman, the recovered addict did not choose this work. Rather, addiction *chose* them. And like the shaman, they work to mend and heal the social fabric. The opioid epidemic would have claimed thousands of more lives if not for the quiet dedication and tireless efforts of recovered addicts all across the United States. It is largely their work that keeps the epidemic from being even more devastating than it is.

Luigi Zoja, in his book *Drugs, Addiction, and Initiation: the Modern Search for Ritual*, argues that the lack of meaningful ritual in modern societies is largely due to our pathological fear of death. We deny the reality of death. Instead, we pursue a fantasy of uninterrupted growth (Zoja 2000). This means that we no longer know how to usher one another through life's transitions; that we do not understand how to facilitate transformation. In pre-modern cultures, marriage, warfare, and the onset of puberty were sacred events. They marked a transition from one state of being to another, the death of one identity and the birth of a new one. These events are no longer sacred—the combat vet is expected to return to life as though nothing happened, marriage can be terminated by simply filling out a few forms, and puberty is regarded as more of a trial for parents and teachers than as a passage to adulthood.

However, the initiatory impulse lives on. It can be seen in gang membership, in the pursuit of extreme sports, and in the dynamics of drug abuse. Getting high is itself often highly ritualized. Many addicts carefully attend to set and setting (e.g., lighting, music) before they imbibe. Bars resemble temples in striking ways—there is an altar, behind which stands a priest who accepts an offering before he dispenses the sacrament. The sacramental liquid causes a felt change in consciousness. It may give you courage or make you amorous. It may even lead you to confess your darkest secrets or deepest wishes to the priest or one of your fellow worshippers.

For addicts, rebirth is achieved through the euphoria of intoxication; sobriety is the land of the dead. Addicts get high to escape the wasteland of ordinary life. When they sober up, they find themselves in an even more debased state. As the condition progresses they become increasingly desperate—they must use more and more to find their way back to the bliss of rebirth.

Recovered addicts have successfully negotiated the world of addiction. They have suffered a life-threatening illness (i.e., opiate addiction), descended into the underworld, and returned as healers. Not only do they have the capacity to help those like themselves, but they can also speak to the societal conditions that give rise to addiction in the first place. They are true authorities; they are the only ones who have the intimate first-hand knowledge of both addiction and recovery.

There are also many *failed initiations.* In these cases, the addicts have descended into the underworld but cannot make their way back. They may relapse or die or they may even achieve lasting sobriety. It is a failed initiation (i.e., dry drunks) if the addicts continue to suffer from RID and/or the mental obsession. These are the addicts who only get sober, but never learn how to regulate stress or deal with negative emotions. They have never really dealt with the demons that drove them to drink in the first place. Unfortunately, this means that their addiction will likely continue to progress along its deadly course. For in the absence of genuine recovery, RID is sure to get worse. If they do not relapse they are likely to develop any number of emotional disorders. Many of these are due to interpersonal problems; others are stress-related or born of a deep and persistent sense of meaninglessness. Needless to say, these people do not know how to help their fellow addicts heal; the most they can offer are techniques or strategies to maintain sobriety.

Recovered addicts are relatively asymptomatic because they have achieved a high degree of integration in their lives. Psycho-social integration is essential to the well-being of individuals and communities. Its presence or absence is likely a determining factor in the etiology and course of many mental disorders. For example, the work of Dr. Edward Tick, a veteran's advocate and author of *Warrior's Return,* shows that psycho-spiritual integration can heal or even prevent soldiers from suffering combat related post-traumatic stress disorder (PTSD) (Tick 2014).

The Vietnamese people enjoy a much higher degree of psycho-social integration than we do in the United States. Familial bonds are especially strong. If a person lost her family during the war, she would almost certainly be spiritually adopted by the larger community. In Vietnamese culture it is taken for granted that the wounds suffered by individuals will be borne by the whole community. There are national days of mourning and pagodas dedicated to the well-being of the souls of the dead. Veterans are encouraged to share their war experience through the practice of communal storytelling. These values and rituals serve to bring people together in times of crisis and to facilitate healing afterward.

Amazingly, these same practices serve a prophylactic function relative to the onset of combat PTSD. Tick cites the research of Dr. Le Van Hao of the National Institute of Psychology in Vietnam. Hao's research team studied the mental health of North Vietnamese combat veterans. They concluded that among North Vietnamese veterans there was "no evidence of combat-induced post traumatic stress disorder and none of the troublesome symptomatology plaguing American veterans" (Tick 2014). Tick's work in his nonprofit organization, Soldier's Heart, uses similar techniques (i.e., storytelling and ritual) to help veterans heal. Tick believes, as do we, that community and meaning are balms to the wounded soul.

Tick's findings also strongly support Dislocation Theory. Both Tick and Alexander show that strong communal ties and shared spiritual values can actually prevent the onset of certain disorders (i.e., PTSD and addiction). They also maintain that meaningful connection is essential to healing. They do not conceive of addiction and PTSD in purely biological terms. Rather, they are *soul pathologies*. This is the reason why they are so responsive to spiritual modalities that foster connection.

Drug abuse itself can be understood as a misdirected spiritual impulse. This was Carl Jung's belief. He argued that the alcoholic's desire for unending bliss is essentially a "mystical thirst"—a desire for union or oneness with God. This may be why the 12 Steps succeed where so many other modalities fail. They address that same desire—the deepest longing of the human being—to know God. At the same time, they validate the perennial truth of the great religious traditions—that the love of God and the love of neighbor are really two sides of the same coin.

13

WHAT IS SUCCESS?

How do we measure success? What are the analytics that are being used in the war against addiction?

Modern society has come to expect data or stats to prove whether or not something is effective or successful. Whether it's sports, business, politics, or health care, we crave stats. But when it comes to recovery, success is a highly subjective term and is extremely hard to quantify.

ONLY A SMALL PERCENTAGE SEEK OR RECEIVE HELP

The industry generally claims, as a rule, that 30% of people who go through substance abuse treatment remain abstinent for a year. We think that number is grossly inflated.

"The therapeutic community claims a 30% success rate, but they only count people who complete the program," Joseph A. Califano Jr., founder of the National Center on Addiction and Substance Abuse and a former U.S. Secretary of Health, Education and Welfare, told *TIME* magazine in 2013. "Seventy to eighty percent drop out in three to six months."

Father John Hardin, chair of the board of trustees at St. Anthony's, a social-services foundation with an addiction-recovery program in San Francisco, puts it more bluntly: "Success for us is that a person hasn't died."[1]

There are an estimated 20 million addicts in the United States, but only 10% of them will ever receive treatment. Finding a bed in the throes of the current opioid epidemic is difficult in the best of circumstances and impossible in the worst. Insurance doesn't always cover treatment and many parts of the country lack the capacity to meet the overwhelming demand in the age of the opioid crisis.

The mental health system is more accessible than drug treatment, although it is also sorely lacking in resources. According to the federal Substance Abuse and Mental Health Services Administration (SAMHSA), there were roughly 20 million people age 12 and over who reported having experienced depression in 2017. Of those, about 12.8 million received treatment.[2] That is over 60%—a far higher rate than those receiving substance abuse services.

SAMHSA's 2017 National Survey on Drug Use and Health found that nearly 21 million people (roughly 1 in 13) who were 12 years of age or older needed treatment for drug or alcohol abuse. Only four million of them actually received treatment. Only a little more than half of those people were treated at a facility specializing in substance abuse.[3]

While it is alarming that such a small percentage of people can access either mental health or substance abuse services, it is especially distressing that the treatment rate for those in need of only drug or alcohol treatment remains so low, especially given the current state of the opioid epidemic. While we don't believe the government is going to be the entity that solves our society's addiction crisis, this is one clear area where it can devote resources to help the cause.

LACK OF QUALITY TREATMENT FACILITIES

The inadequate number of treatment beds is a major issue, but the issue of quality of treatment almost never comes up. The guidelines provided by SAMHSA and the National Institute on Drug Abuse (NIDA) are vague and generic.

Here are the principles that NIDA maintains should form the basis of any effective treatment program:[4]

- Addiction is a complex but treatable disease that affects brain function and behavior
- No single treatment is right for everyone

- People need to have quick access to treatment
- Effective treatment addresses all of the patient's needs, not just his or her drug use
- Staying in treatment long enough is critical
- Counseling and other behavioral therapies are the most commonly used forms of treatment
- Medications are often an important part of treatment, especially when combined with behavioral therapies
- Treatment plans must be reviewed often and modified to fit the patient's changing needs
- Treatment should address other possible mental disorders
- Medically assisted detoxification is only the first stage of treatment
- Treatment doesn't need to be voluntary to be effective
- Drug use during treatment must be monitored continuously
- Treatment programs should test patients for HIV/AIDS, hepatitis B and C, tuberculosis, and other infectious diseases, as well as teach them about steps they can take to reduce their risk of these illnesses

And NIDA recommends the following treatments for addiction:

- Behavioral counseling
- Medication
- Medical devices and applications used to treat withdrawal symptoms or deliver skills training
- Evaluation and treatment for co-occurring mental health issues such as depression and anxiety
- Long-term follow-up to prevent relapse

DEFINING SUCCESS

According to SAMHSA, success is defined by whether the addict:

- Stops using drugs
- Stays drug-free
- Is productive in the family, at work, and in society

The truth is, there is no standardized method of measuring the success of treatment. Most facilities only use quantitative measurements, that is, they only measure lengths of sobriety. Some facilities base their metrics on how many people completed the program, sobriety rates immediately post-treatment, client interviews, and internal studies. Generally speaking, little distinction is ever made between recovery and sobriety. Qualitative factors (e.g., overall quality of life) are almost never taken into account. Consumers are right to be skeptical about such data.

While these approaches and metrics are rational, they actually tell us very little. As we have stressed throughout this book, many people achieve sobriety but continue to decompensate emotionally and/or interpersonally. Many wind up in psychiatric care. We believe that the only reliable way to judge whether someone is doing well is to observe their involvement in the local recovery community. And of course, that is practically impossible to quantify.

While some treatment centers provide stats, the fact is that there is no consensus as to what constitutes success. Is a client *successful* if he or she remains sober for one year, five years, 10 years, 20 years? Is he or she successful if they get a job, finish college, have children, or buy a home? If these things are indicators of success, how are we to understand relapse?

Our network, Granite Recovery Centers, like many others, does not track recidivism/relapse numbers. For starters, the cost of a quality study would be prohibitive. It would also be incredibly difficult to track down every client that came through our doors. Even if we were able to track down a large percentage of our clients post-treatment, the data would still be extremely unreliable because it would depend on self-reporting. Unless we tracked everyone down and gave them surprise drug tests, we couldn't confirm abstinence and would be providing unreliable data.

In addition, many addicts in recovery do not want to answer surveys. They are simply too busy living their lives, while many simply may not want to look backward. The addicts who have relapsed or are not doing well, meanwhile, would likely be untruthful, which would skew the data as well.

Successful treatment is much easier to quantify with other medical conditions. In the case of cancer treatment, success equals remission.

Treatment for diabetes is measured in terms of blood sugar. With addiction, success is vaguely or rarely defined. This is probably the main reason why so many facilities and research institutions use sobriety as the baseline measure.

If someone is receiving medication-assisted treatment (MAT) (i.e., Suboxone or Methadone), are they in recovery? We would say they are not. We will discuss these treatments at length in the next chapter but suffice it to say that we believe these drugs have value in a detox setting and as a part of any overall harm reduction strategy. But they are opioids; and we emphatically deny that someone can be in recovery from opiate addiction while they are taking opioids.

What constitutes success is ultimately a personal matter. Ask yourself the question, what do you want for your life? If getting off of opiates is too daunting a prospect at this time in your life, then maybe MAT is for you. It may help you stabilize, find employment, or reunite with your family. If your goal is to be off opiates and still drink alcohol or smoke pot, then that is what you should try to do. These may be successful outcomes for some people. It is all a matter of intention. But success is not necessarily the same thing as recovery.

Dr. John Kelly, Professor of Psychiatry in the Field of Addiction Medicine at Harvard Medical School and founder of the Recovery Research Institute at Massachusetts General Hospital, defines *success* like this: "Recovery from a substance-use disorder is defined as a process of improved physical, psychological, and social well-being and health after having suffered from a substance-related condition."[5]

This definition makes sense to us. It is holistic. It recognizes that recovery is a process and that it occurs simultaneously in multiple domains. It does not assert that "relapse is part of recovery."

Our version of success includes a belief that there is such a thing as real recovery. It is based in abstinence, but abstinence isn't the milestone—it's the foundation.

These are other key indicators of success:

- The person demonstrates that they've changed
- He or she practices honesty

- His or her personal relationships are in good shape
- He or she demonstrates the ability to deal with adversity and frustration

Of course, everyone has problems, before, after, and during addiction, so we are not saying that someone has not succeeded if he or she is struggling in their marriage. But difficulties in these areas should be considered commonplace and in line with social norms.

Recovered addicts and alcoholics can and do lead purposeful lives. They're profoundly grateful and are excited about life. Their character and integrity are important to them.

Some may think these indicators sound like a *pink cloud*. The so-called pink cloud phenomenon is fairly common in early recovery. It refers to the newly sober person who is enjoying some of the secondary gains of recovery (i.e., sound sleep, improved financial status, a healthy diet). Enjoyment of these pleasures can lull the addict into a false sense of security. They are not reliable indicators of recovery; most of them simply follow from being sober for a given length of time.

We have discussed the breakthrough that happens when the addict realizes that his problem wasn't drugs or alcohol; that getting high was merely symptomatic of something much deeper. The pink cloud syndrome may temporarily obscure the reality of RID—restless, irritable, and discontent—but it won't be long before life starts throwing curveballs.

How well addicts deal with adversity is the ultimate measure of recovery. How do they deal with failure, loss, or rejection? Recovery is an *inside job*—it is ultimately about the addict's internal condition. A person can be recovered and homeless, recovered and HIV positive, or recovered and incarcerated. One can have meaningful relationships in prison. One can practice rigorous honesty living in a shelter. Recovery can be achieved in virtually any situation if addicts are honest and earnest and there are recovered addicts there to help them. We know a recovered alcoholic who has taken men on death row through the 12 Steps. The Oxford Group used to say, "Man's extremity is God's opportunity."

There are still other indicators of success. If a recovered addict tells you he is going to do something, you can be sure he will follow through with it. Recovered addicts will be abstinent; they will practice self-care and will lead productive lives. Most important, they will devote part of their spare time to helping addicts. Recovered addicts are out in the trenches, working shoulder to shoulder with boots on the ground, intervening directly in the lives of those seeking recovery. They do their homework and spread the message. They may be sponsors, volunteers, or activists. Alcoholism and addiction are characterized by selfishness, therefore, selflessness and altruism are the ultimate indicators of recovery. How they spend their spare time and spare change reveals a lot about their spiritual conditions.

INNOVATION AND ACTIVISM

While we support lobbying efforts and have discussed the need for informed activism to shape policy, we do not believe the solution will come from above. This is why we are adamant that we must form a tribe. We need to address the crisis from the ground up. We need to assume that we are not going to be rescued. This means that we have to be creative and flexible. If we all, as members of the tribe, brought our various skill sets and resources to the table, there is no telling what we might achieve.

Here are some of the tactics we endorse:

- Research and conversation
- Use of social media
- Education and professionalization
- Public speaking
- Entrepreneurial initiative

As we have already noted, it is imperative that we do our research and share our findings with one another. We need to be reading the same books and listening to the same speakers. It may not be readily apparent, but research and conversation is actually one of the more subversive things we can do. It builds community from the ground up; it disseminates information from one person to another. And it all happens under the radar.

Social media is a powerful means of disseminating information and building broad-based networks with like-minded people at home and abroad. Join online groups that share your interests; become a digital activist. Use your Facebook page to spread information. Start a podcast and spread the message of the tribe.

We need tribal members to get advanced degrees so that they can position themselves to be of maximum service to the cause. One might become a clinician (i.e., PsyD, MSW, PhD, MA) or pursue a career in law or in one of any number of medical professions. Clergy (MDiv) are also uniquely positioned to make a difference in the lives of addicts. One could also pursue certification as a yoga teacher or some type of somatic practitioner. Use your education as a platform—share what you learn. Write research papers, online blogs, articles, and books.

Members of the tribe must be vocal. Take it upon yourself to speak to any audience that will listen to what you have to say. You must not confine your efforts to AA or NA. And it is imperative that you not be reticent when it comes to controversial topics like the war on drugs or the medication of children. Speak your truth. Remember, we do not have the same financial resources as our opponents. We have to do our own legwork.

Think outside of the box. Start a business that employs addicts in early recovery. Open a sober living house. Start a rideshare or a babysitting co-op for people in recovery. Volunteer as a group at the Veterans Administration or at your local animal shelter. Remember that people are watching. The civilian world needs to know that there are thousands of recovered addicts making a difference in the lives of their communities.

These are the strategies of *integration*. This is what it looks like when we wed 12-Step Spirituality and Dislocation Theory.

Statistics aside, we are witnessing the birth of a new movement. It is still young—but it is real. Our hope is that this book will serve as an impetus to do research, converse, and organize. We are already seeing the beginning of a snowball effect—it is inspiring.

A CALL TO ARMS

At this point, you should have a good sense of the nature of addiction and the forces that cause and perpetuate it. You know what it means to be recovered and why we believe it to be the gold standard of recovery.

Society doesn't have a clear picture of addiction or recovery. Their views have been shaped by the media, by those with a vested interest in promoting the idea that the addict is always in a precarious state of *recovering*. Relapse is regarded as something of an inevitability—a part of recovery.

When people meet someone in recovery (or better yet, recovered) from opiate addiction, they often say things like, "Oh, that must be so hard for you," or "You must have to battle every day."

But the truth is, if you are recovered, it is not hard at all. It is not a battle. The media and academia would have you believe that we are just barely hanging on. The prevailing wisdom is that recovery is a chore and that maintaining sobriety is a matter of *white knuckling* it through life.

But that's not even close to the truth. The *Big Book* tells us that we can go anywhere anyone can go if our "spiritual house is in order" and if we have good reason for being there. That is why Piers can safely administer morphine to his dying father. Or why Eric can make amends with someone who is still getting high. Or why both of them have done numerous 12-Step calls at the homes of people who are still actively smoking coke or drinking vodka. We have attended wedding receptions and gone to Christmas and New Year's Eve parties. We can take trips to Las Vegas, Miami, New York, and are comfortable being around partiers. We do not need to bring an AA friend or make sure that we have a pocket full of phone numbers. This is the great promise of the *Big Book*. We are living proof that it is true. We are proud of our recovery and we enjoy life, far more than we ever did using.

Certainly, as recovered addicts we have suffered our share of trauma. We still do. It goes with the territory. If you work with addicts, you are going to get your heart broken—repeatedly.

It rattles you to your core when you find out that the client you spoke to on Friday died two days later. It is gut-wrenching to speak with parents who have lost a child, or to contemplate the pain of a motherless child. And it is impossible to find words for the parent who has lost multiple children. These experiences are day-to-day realities for those on the front lines of the opioid epidemic.

Over time, you become calloused and battle fatigued. You become somewhat desensitized, but not in a cold or uncaring way. It's a survival mechanism. It's simply what happens when you deal with suffering at this magnitude. It's an intense job and it can take a heavy toll. Self-care is of paramount importance but, unfortunately, most of us have to learn that the hard way.

On the other hand, it can be the most rewarding work imaginable. You cannot bear witness to real recovery and at the same time doubt the reality of God. There is nothing like watching a young woman get sober, find recovery, and get her children back. Nothing like the heartfelt hug of gratitude one gets from a long-suffering parent. Nothing like seeing a client a year later and having to do a double take because even though you remember her name, you can't place her face. Sometimes the transformations are almost impossible to believe, even after you have witnessed them time and again.

We are seeking to build a tribe that is led by a diverse group of recovered addicts, people who are willing to dedicate themselves to serving others. The thing about war is—it doesn't sleep. War doesn't take a vacation. If you let your guard down or you get complacent, you can lose the battle. In this conflict, taking a break at the wrong time can, and often does, result in a loss of life. More than ever before, we are being asked to make great personal sacrifices for the sake of recovery. Nothing less will suffice. We need to work with addicts, keep up with our research, and spread the message every day, 365 days a year. What we can never achieve as individuals over the short term, we can accomplish together over the course of years. This responsibility is the price of recovery. Our passion is our greatest asset.

Remember: recovered addicts have stamina. We have skin in the game—way more than the opposition, who are largely motivated by profit. We are in it for the long haul and we plan on leaving it all on the field. That's why we decided to write this book. It's a call to arms. We need to do more. We need to try harder. *But if we come together, we might very well achieve the impossible.*

NOTES

1. http://ideas.time.com/2013/04/03/we-need-to-rethink-rehab/ ("Viewpoint: We Need to Rethink Rehab," *TIME* magazine, April 3, 2013.)
2. https://www.samhsa.gov/data/report/2017-nsduh-annual-national-report
3. https://www.samhsa.gov/data/report/2017-nsduh-annual-national-report
4. https://www.drugabuse.gov/publications/drugfacts/treatment-approaches-drug-addiction (National Institute on Drug Abuse)
5. https://www.recoveryanswers.org/recovery-101/

14

HOW TO CHOOSE A
TREATMENT CENTER

By now the reader should understand why we are strong advocates for 12-Step recovery. It is a tried-and-true method that has shown itself capable of delivering the best possible outcome. This is not to say that it always works or that it's the right fit for everyone. But it is a sound abstinence-based method that has freed thousands upon thousands of addicts from the obsession to use.

Consumers should not take anything for granted when exploring treatment options. Many treatment centers identify themselves as "12 Step." Very few, however, actually practice the steps. Most only bring clients to AA meetings or invite AA members to speak in-house. While we support those practices, we strongly believe that the best time to commence step work is immediately after detox. It is, after all, the precedent set by AA's founders.

We are strong advocates of the *Big Book*. It is the original and most widely used 12-Step manual. Ideally, clients should do the first seven steps out of the *Big Book* while in residential treatment. This has many advantages, the main one being that completion of seven steps usually brings with it a palpable sense of relief. Many addicts only buy into step work after they have begun to feel better. Clients who finish steps four and five leave treatment with a sense of accomplishment. They have a strong foundation and a sense of direction; they know what they need to do moving forward.

Facilitation of the 12 Steps is more of an art than a technique. It is not something that can be learned in a weekend workshop or certification program. Treatment centers should be led by talented 12-Step practitioners—recovered addicts with extensive experience using the steps to meet the trials of everyday life. Recovered addicts are preeminently suited to serve those in early recovery. This is a contentious issue, but we beg the reader to look at outcomes. There are thousands of recovered addicts with extensive track records in helping addicts achieve permanent recovery. There is nothing comparable in the world of psychiatry. Recovered addicts are numerically significant, yet, our existence is either ignored or denied by the media, clinical world, and academia.

THE APPROPRIATE STAFF

In light of the previous information, we believe that a quality treatment center should be staffed primarily by people in recovery. Solid recovery should be evident throughout the ranks, from line staff to upper management. Ideally, many former clients will be employed at the facility. These employees have an intimate understanding of the program—its philosophy and rationale. They also often have more *street cred* with clients than do more senior employees.

A good treatment center will have a stellar clinical team. The entire clinical staff should be 12-Step savvy. Unfortunately, such people are hard to find. Most substance abuse clinicians have only a superficial knowledge of the 12 Steps. In fact, we know of no graduate program in counseling or social work that teaches anything of significance about AA, its history, or the efficacy and dynamics of step work. The reality of the recovered addict is completely ignored. These programs usually only identify AA as the progenitor of the self-help movement. (While *meeting-maker AA* passes for self-help, the 12 Steps do not. The steps are for people who cannot help themselves; addicts and alcoholics are, according to the *Big Book*, beyond the reach of human power.)

The clinical team is indispensable in treating those addicts who suffer from other serious emotional symptoms and mental disorders. Some of the more common conditions and behaviors seen in addicts and alcoholics include: eating disorders, dementia, substance-induced psychosis, suicidal ideation, and self-injurious behavior. The clinical team also provides invaluable support to clients who are writing their fourth steps (make a searching and fearless moral inventory of yourself). Writing a fourth step is a strenuous and soul-searching exercise. Often, addicts have to revisit a lot of potentially re-traumatizing material. This is a major reason why step work is best done in a residential setting under the care and supervision of a team of clinicians and seasoned step practitioners. Taking steps in a communal setting affords a level of intimacy and mutual understanding that cannot be replicated on the outside.

It is important that the staff stay abreast of what's happening in the world of addiction. We cannot overstate this point. The recovery world is decidedly insular. It has little or no interest in contextualizing the phenomena of addiction. Historical and socioeconomic factors are almost completely ignored. We endorse Dislocation Theory because it affords the best model to explore addiction from perspectives (e.g. anthropological, economic, historical) beyond the medical model. Staff should be well-informed about issues like Big Pharma, the war on drugs, or the role that stress and trauma play in recovery. Teaching addicts about the societal forces that drive addiction is also highly therapeutic. It helps them make sense of their experience. This kind of knowledge empowers and inspires; it takes recovery to an entirely different level.

COMMUNITY

Clients need to feel safe; they must trust their environment and the people in whose care they have been placed. Establishing trust is not easy. While in active addiction, addicts are continually stressed by the demands of getting money to buy drugs. In all likelihood they are also contending with issues ranging from poor health to legal issues and marital conflict. Their only respite is in getting high. Unfortunately, treatment also induces stress. Clients find themselves suddenly living among strangers in a new and bewildering environment. Their problems come crashing down on them and they can no longer find relief by getting high. Building community in these circumstances is a tall order.

Many treatment centers adopt a confrontational approach. This is usually done for the sake of accountability with the rationale being that addicts must stop blaming others and come to understand that their actions have consequences. While we agree with this in theory, we believe it should be tempered with a more nuanced, trauma-informed approach. Treatment centers must make every effort to treat clients with kindness and respect. This does not mean that there shouldn't be consequences for antisocial behavior. But providers need to learn how to maintain strong boundaries without being overly rigid or inflexible. We should never re-traumatize the already-traumatized by shaming them or subjecting them to gratuitous criticism or punishment.

Addicts must learn how to regulate stress. Relaxation optimizes neuroplasticity. All treatment centers should avail themselves of somatic practices that bring clients to states of deep relaxation. There should be regularly scheduled yoga or tai chi classes. There should also be a strong emphasis on prayer and meditation. Ideally, clients will leave treatment convinced of the efficacy of these disciplines. These services can go a long way toward helping clients develop their own daily practice. Learning the basics of self-care should be a primary treatment goal.

FAMILY SUPPORT

There should also be a robust family program. We feel that staff-family communication is an essential part of treatment. The family is usually the best source of collateral information and their reports are almost always more reliable than those provided by clients. Furthermore, most families need to be coached on how to best deal with their loved ones as they move through treatment. The fact that addicts are adept at manipulating families goes without saying. Unfortunately, our loved ones often labor under the delusion that they are responsible for our addiction or that they can somehow determine (for better or worse) the outcome of treatment. Parents and spouses need to understand that there is nothing they can do to guarantee success. The most they can do is help create circumstances that are the most conducive to recovery; this starts with honesty. Others who are affected must learn to be truthful and forthright; they need to be reassured that it is okay to express emotions like fear and anger, and that the addict needs to come to terms with the harm he or she has caused others.

In addition to regular staff-family communication, the treatment center should also offer a variety of family groups. At Granite Recovery Centers (GRC) we ask family members to attend orientation. Family orientation serves to explain our treatment modality and aftercare services. It affords an opportunity for question and answer sessions. We also offer a more in-depth, bi-monthly family workshop and a weekly support meeting. These are open to the public. The weekly support meeting splits into two smaller groups: one is an open discussion group, the other a step workshop for family members. We believe that we cannot hope to meet the opioid crisis without the help of families and friends. Anyone who is affected by the addict's situation is an invaluable yet largely untapped resource. Many of those who are affected are actively seeking ways to serve addicts and/or the people who love them.

MEDICATION-ASSISTED TREATMENT (MAT)

There is a great deal of controversy surrounding MAT. The medications in question most often are Suboxone and Methadone. Suboxone is widely touted as the gold standard for treating opioid addiction. Methadone is an opioid agonist. This means that, like heroin, it binds with the mu-opioid receptor in the brain. Using methadone for *opioid maintenance therapy* amounts to substituting one drug for another. Suboxone is a combination of two drugs: buprenorphine (a partial opioid agonist) and naloxone (a pure opioid antagonist). Because it is a partial agonist, Suboxone also delivers a small opioid dose to the brain's mu receptor. This makes it highly addictive. Naloxone is a pure opioid antagonist. It prevents additional agonists from reaching the receptor. When an opioid addict takes Suboxone, they experience relief from withdrawal symptoms by virtue of the agonist (buprenorphine). The naloxone serves to prevent the addict from getting high should they take more opioids. (This only lasts for the duration of the dose, which for buprenorphine is at most 37 hours.)

We believe that Suboxone is an effective detox and harm reduction drug. However, we strenuously object to its designation as a form of treatment. Suboxone and methadone are highly addictive, despite the public narrative to the contrary. Withdrawal symptoms are every bit as painful as those experienced by heroin addicts. Fear of withdrawal leads many people to stay on these medications for years. Opioid dependence does not constitute treatment for opioid addiction. Furthermore, Suboxone is widely abused. Many addicts use it between heroin runs. Other addicts report that they abuse other drugs (e.g., Adderall or cocaine) while being "treated" with Suboxone. Suboxone is also the number one drug of abuse in the prison system ("prison heroin"). The program at GRC is an abstinence-based program and these drugs are used only during a six-day detox. Our clients almost never advocate for the use of Suboxone or methadone. They do, however, frequently speak out against it.

There are numerous reports of long-term Suboxone use being linked to hair and tooth loss as well as adrenal imbalances. However, the veracity of these claims is denied by Reckitt Benckiser, the manufacturer of Suboxone. Be that as it may, there are thousands of addicts who want to get off of MAT. If you want to get a sense of the scope of the problem, Google "how to get off Suboxone." You'll get millions of results with all sorts of information, some factual, some not.[1]

Suboxone is now widely promoted as the only real option for opioid addicts. We are now hearing that *abstinence kills* and that failure to refer opioid addicts to Suboxone providers should be grounds for medical malpractice. Advocates of abstinence-based treatment are likened to flat earthers. We are painted out as stubborn, deniers of science, old-fashioned, or worse. Needless to say, this kind of hyperbole and name calling does nothing to further the debate and is counterproductive to fighting this epidemic.

Advocates for Suboxone frequently claim that MAT is evidence-based best practice. However, we believe that many of these studies that are cited to support this claim are actually quite weak, if not flagrantly deceptive.

For example, in 2015 the National Institute on Drug Abuse (NIDA) re-leased an article titled, *Long-Term Follow-Up of Medication-Assisted Treatment for Addiction to Pain Relievers Yields "Cause for Optimism."* It cited the "Prescription Opioid Addiction Treatment Study," that claimed a 61% *success rate* for Suboxone over a period of 3.5 years. However, the study had serious flaws. To begin with, researchers were only able to find 338 of the 635 original participants at the end of 42 months. This is a participant loss of over 53%. Furthermore, the study's claims were based on participants' responses to the following question, "Have you used your drug of choice in the last 30 days?" A recovery success rate of 61% was based on 206 respondents answering "no." Needless to say, this study tells us next to nothing and looks to be a good example of confirmation bias. It is troubling to consider how such shoddy research is being used to jus-tify the diversion of billions of taxpayer dollars to Big Pharma in order to "treat" the opioid epidemic.

More troubling still is the lack of shared terminology. This article takes recovery to mean abstinence from one's "drug of choice" (presumably an opiate) for a period of 30 days at the end of 42 months of medication-assisted treatment. The article also tacitly assumes that someone can be in recovery from opioids even while abusing other drugs. (Meaning some-one can be in *recovery* from opioid addiction even while abusing cocaine and alcohol.) This strange idea is now widely taught in graduate schools around the country. Fortunately, it is rarely heard in residential treatment programs and almost never in 12-Step meetings. In those settings it is mostly still accepted that *a drug is a drug* and that someone cannot be in recovery from one substance while still abusing another.

It should be noted that prior to 2000, methadone clinics were the only facilities that could legally prescribe opioids to "treat" narcotic addiction. That changed with the passage of the Drug Addiction Treatment Act. Now any qualified physician can treat opioid dependence with schedule III-V narcotics (including Suboxone). This effectively reversed the 1914 Harrison Act, which criminalized the prescribing of opiates to maintain addicts' addictions.

Readers should also understand that the treatment of chronic pain and mental illness are a big part of what is driving up the cost of healthcare.

Nearly a quarter of all Americans are on Medicaid. Since 2016, Congress has had to divert funds from Social Security retirement to the Social Security disability trust fund. Increasing numbers of Americans are being forced to seek federal benefits as their employers can no longer meet those costs; hence, the explosion of part-time employment. A large percentage of disability claimants are receiving benefits for pain and/or mental illness. The prescription of psychiatric drugs and pain meds are a big part of what is driving up medical costs. At the same time, we are being bombarded with propaganda that insists that untreated pain and mental illness are major public health problems.

ACCESS TO TREATMENT

Given the preceding information, the reader may be surprised to learn that as of 2015, only one in five opiate addicts could access treatment.[2] Furthermore, as of 2015, Medicaid only covered MAT (i.e., methadone, naltrexone, and Suboxone) in 28 states. Of late, there has been a strong push for expansion of Medicaid reimbursement for MAT. At the same time, there has been no real increase in public funding of residential abstinence-based treatment. In most states, Medicaid reimbursement for residential treatment is less than $200 a day. That rate is simply too low to cover operating costs. We contend that the current push for MAT has less to do with efficacy and outcome than the concerted effort of lobbyists on Capitol Hill. Advocates for abstinence-based therapy do not have a huge war chest, but Big Pharma does.

FREE SERVICES

The integrity of a treatment center is most evident in its willingness to provide free services to those in need. At GRC we provide scholarships for select clients. We have also dedicated the Pritts Recovery Center (PRC) to the larger community. PRC hosts special events as well as a monthly *Big Book* workshop. We also have a regular weekly menu of groups that include a family support group, several 12-Step meetings, a recovery workshop, and a yoga class. All events are free and open to the public. Consumers should always ask providers if they offer free services to the public. The answer will reveal a lot about the leadership and mission of the treatment center.

AFTERCARE

A quality treatment center will also provide quality aftercare. Ideally, a client will go from primary treatment to a residential extended-care facility. Extended care provides the same services (i.e., 12-Step facilitation and clinical) as primary treatment, but in a less restrictive environment. Over time, the client will be given greater freedom. His leash will get longer and longer; he will get a cell phone, a vehicle, and eventually, a job. Too often, clients who go straight from residential treatment to sober living find themselves overwhelmed by various temptations or the stresses of having to find a job and pay bills. Quality extended care also provides support and direction to clients as they negotiate the ninth step amends process. Many addicts relapse around step nine. Having done the hard work of Steps 1 through 7, they often *take a break* before starting amends. This can be deadly. The relief that follows reading a fifth step conspires with the fear of making amends. The addict squeezes the lemon of feeling good until there is nothing left and relapses in short order—relapse almost always being the result of failing to make amends.

Finally, a good treatment center cultivates a strong sense of community. It recognizes the value of alumni relations. At GRC, we refer our clients to sponsors we know and trust. We also invite our former clients to return to the facility to share their experience and hear fifth steps. We work hard to build relationships with families, sympathetic clinicians, and members of the law enforcement and academic communities. Over time we have succeeded in building a strong recovery community throughout New England and beyond. We hope this community will form the nucleus of a new movement.

NOTES

1. https://www.thefix.com/content/hard-to-kick-suboxone?page=all
2. https://www.theatlantic.com/health/archive/2015/10/why-80 -percent-of-addicts-cant-get-treatment/410269/

15

THE MISSION OF THE TRIBE

We've talked in this book about the root causes of addiction, the many societal forces that push addicts deeper into the void. We have also told you a bit about ourselves, our respective recoveries, and our work with addicts. But really, this book is about forming a tribe—a tribe of like-minded people who have found recovery and want to share their gifts with the world; a tribe that wants to serve and educate; a tribe of activists whose work is rooted in spirituality and knowledge.

We believe that sobriety and recovery are two very different things. What we are focused on is helping people find what we call *real recovery*. Everyday, someone in AA celebrates a sobriety milestone. Addicts are given a chip that marks their length of sobriety, whether that be days, months, or years. This is an inspiring experience for addicts who were once held captive by drugs or alcohol. It's even more amazing for their loved ones. It is a highlight of the AA meeting experience.

But these chips only represent days/weeks/months/years sober. Not everyone who gets a chip is recovered—or even recovering. In fact, there is a widely held belief in the recovery community (and the world at large) that no one is ever recovered. Instead, it is taken for granted that anyone with an extended sobriety is simply recovering.

We disagree. *We have recovered.* We are no longer riddled with the mental obsession. We have moved beyond sobriety to find meaning and purpose in our lives. We do not believe that "meetings are our medicine" and that we must stay huddled in fear and fellowship every night of our lives. Instead, we go to meetings to serve others—to practice the twelfth step. And we do it without using any of the maintenance drugs that we discussed in previous chapters.

RECOVERED—RATHER THAN RECOVERING

We do not use medicinal marijuana or any other addictive substances or medications (e.g., Ativan, Kratom, Tramadol) to cope with the void left by opioids or alcohol. Instead, we strive to make meaningful connections (in and out of the world of recovery) with our fellow human beings to combat the dislocation that's destroying our society; fueling addiction; and ratcheting up fear, anxiety, and depression.

Being sober is not a penalty—it is a gift. And we embrace it every day. Do we still acknowledge our anniversary dates? Of course we do. It is important to commemorate the beginning of our journey, the day when we decided to stop poisoning our bodies and minds.

But at some point after we began to work the steps, something *clicked* and we felt a degree of relief that we had not believed possible. It no longer felt like we were doing time. We were suddenly intensely curious about recovery and where it might lead us. Only from the perspective of relief could we finally see that drugs were not our problem—not really—they were but a symptom. The problem was far more sinister. It lay within us and around us, rooted in feelings of insecurity, alienation, fear, and meaninglessness. We weren't comfortable in our own skin and we weren't comfortable around others. We needed drugs and alcohol to get through the day.

Once we had the breakthrough, we were energized to finish the steps and to serve others. Many of us were surprised to find that we actually enjoyed helping others! And to witness one's own recovery replicated in another addict was the most powerful experience of all. It brought it all back home. We understood that we were recovered and had been given the power to help others recover. Recovered is something that can be achieved, over and over.

SERVICE—INSIDE AND OUTSIDE THE HALLS

As the years passed, we found that we were hungry for more. We came to understand what Bill Wilson meant when he likened AA to "spiritual kindergarten." So we read widely and explored a variety of spiritual disciplines. We eventually went pro and institutionalized step work. And all the while we pondered why the problem was getting worse, exponentially worse. Now we are ready to share what we have learned.

This is the mission of the tribe: *To get into the trenches and stay in the trenches.* We have discussed how AA is rooted in anonymity and how meetings are not venues where addicts can discuss and debate issues like medication-assisted treatment (MAT) or the war on drugs. Meeting halls are hallowed ground for many AA members, and we respect that. We agree that we must take pains to honor the AA traditions, but the mission extends far beyond the 12-Step world. If the mission of the tribe is to be realized, then we must move out of church basements and VFW halls and journey out into the streets. The trenches extend far beyond these meeting halls and are much larger than the important one-on-one work between addicts. We must go to detox facilities and prisons and psych wards. And we must carry our message to the public at large, especially to educators, law enforcement, government officials, and medical personnel.

As members of the tribe, we do not need to remain anonymous. In fact, we need to let people know who we are and how to find us. We need to let folks know about the great work that is being done—and that recovery is not only possible, but is a reality. Thousands of people are getting better despite being in the midst of the worst drug epidemic this country has ever seen.

ERIC SHARES HIS STORY

Eric recently met with some firefighters in Derry, NH. The purpose of the meeting was twofold: (1) to have an open and honest conversation about Narcan and (2) to address the fatigue and frustration of first responders who find themselves administering the life-saving anti-opioid drug night after night, oftentimes to the same person. The firefighters talked openly about how jaded it made them feel to see the same addicts overdosing over and over again. They talked about how Narcan calls dominate their shifts—sometimes even preventing them from responding to other emergencies.

Eric sympathized with their frustration. He then told a story about how he had overdosed in an apartment in Derry. The people he was getting high with dragged him outside and left him on the lawn. Firefighters were called and arrived on the scene, administered a dose of Narcan, and brought Eric back to life—literally. It was Eric's fifth overdose. He told the firefighters he was lucky to be alive.

A firefighter named Rick Fisher was in the audience. He listened intently. When Eric was done speaking, Rick raised his hand and asked Eric a few questions about the year the incident occurred and the whereabouts of the address. Eric answered.

Rick's face turned serious. "That was me," he told Eric. "That was me that helped you that night."

Eric was stunned. Both men's eyes filled up. They walked toward each other, shook hands, and embraced in an emotional hug.

"You saved my life bro," Eric told Rick. "Thank you."

Eric went on to describe what he has done with his recovery. He got clean shortly after that incident and, as of this writing, has been recovered for 12 years. He opened a small sober house that would eventually grow to become Granite Recovery Centers, New England's largest substance abuse treatment network with nearly 300 beds. He's helped thousands of people get clean and has created hundreds of jobs in the field of recovery.

This is the power of being recovered.

THE POWER OF THE RECOVERED ACTIVIST

In order for the recovery movement to grow at scale, it must start one-on-one, and grow from there. What Rick Fisher learned that day was that the overdosed addict, if given a chance to survive and the means to real recovery, can become a powerful force in the lives of other addicts.

For those of us who have recovered from addiction, we always need to be mindful that the next person you help could be the one that's going to change the world. Time and time again, recovered addicts have been blown away by the transformations of those they serve. We have seen severely addicted individuals go from being despondent, desperate, and homeless to being the most highly effective and sought-after sponsors in their home communities. One recovered addict can have a disproportionately positive effect on those around him. A truly recovered addict's reach extends far beyond what would be possible if he or she were merely clean and sober.

Many of us were so wrecked by addiction that we wondered why we were still alive. After we got sober, it was even worse. Life lacked meaning. We could no longer feel pleasure. We had no sense that we would ever enjoy life like we did when the drugs were *working*. So we were shocked to find ourselves revitalized by real recovery. Amazed that life was suddenly so interesting. The passion of recovered addicts is the number one underutilized and unacknowledged resource we have in the battle against addiction. It is time it was properly harnessed and let loose upon the world.

Because the opioid epidemic is getting worse, we must get as many addicts into recovery as possible. This movement starts with recovery; and then we take up the banner of informed activism. The mission is not only about helping people get into recovery, it's also about waking them up to truth.

Informed activism is everything from advocating and lobbying for legislation to taking the time to have coffee with the mom of an addict or the husband of an alcoholic woman. It is about speaking in classrooms or before audiences of EMTs, clinicians, or the incarcerated. Most important, it means doing research and having deep and meaningful conversations. We strongly encourage our readers to read the books written by the authors whose work has shaped our mission. They include (but are not limited to): Carl Hart, Michelle Alexander, Sam Quinones, Nick Reding, Russell Brand, Gabor Mate, Richard Miller, Robert Whitaker, Charles Bowden, and most important, Bruce Alexander. Read these authors, go hear them speak, and watch them on YouTube. Tell others about what you learn. Relate their research to your own experience. Speak the truth. It is up to you.

The goal is to have so many recovered addicts doing this work that they're always within an arm's length of anyone who needs them. We need to form our own network of recovery. We cannot rely upon the government or medical establishment to aid us in our efforts any longer. They are at odds with much of what we believe and do and there are too many competing agendas. We must realize that no one is going to solve these problems for us. We must form our own networks. The tribe must do the work itself.

Seeing this mission and movement unfold and grow is exciting and inspiring. In our little corner of the world in New England, we're deep by the thousands. But the work is never done. The scale of the problem is unbelievable. And we have to face the fact that success will probably only be achieved in decades—not in a few years. It is unlikely that any of us will live to see the end of this war.

A GREATER MISSION

If Bill and Bob—the founders of AA—were alive today, we believe they would understand the rationale behind our mission. While we understand why a lot of people want to remain anonymous—and we respect that fully—we are living in very different times than when the *Big Book* was written. We live in a 24/7 society that is being overwhelmed by the rapidity of technological advancement, economic change, and environmental degradation.

AA's founders had no way of anticipating something like the opiate epidemic that is now killing more people than cancer or car accidents and has actually lowered the life expectancy of adults in America. Had they been armed with this information, would our founders have remained anonymous in church basements? We doubt that they would have.

AA was founded by a stock broker and a doctor looking for a way out of alcoholism. Their thoughts, ideas, and blueprint for getting better are as relevant today as they ever were. But what's happened since then, especially in the past 20 years, is a game changer. This is a crisis of epic proportions. Our families, our co-workers, and our friends are dying in record numbers. We are at war. We cannot *refuse to talk about it.*

The authors of this book are living proof that real recovery is possible. We are both veterans of multiple failed treatments. We both did time in methadone programs. Neither of us could stay sober through meeting attendance alone. We both only finally got better when we embraced and practiced the 12 Steps.

But we did something more. We went pro. As a result, we came to understand many of the forces that prevent addicts from getting better. This led us, in turn, to doing research and more research. Now we have a platform to share what we have learned. And what is most amazing is that the solution is so simple. It is all about connection—connection to God, to one's neighbor, and to one's body and soul. But it is also about connection to knowledge—to the truth of what is really going on. This is what we have been sharing with our clients and friends. This is what our book is all about.

A new breed of recovery is being born. Hardcore addicts and alcoholics, inflamed with passion for recovery, are stepping out of church basements to take up the battle as activists. These are people who have a first-person understanding of what addiction is and what it takes to recover. Being long-term consumers of treatment services, they can speak to what doesn't work as well. They are spiritually hungry and are constantly exploring how to best utilize wellness and somatic practices to enhance and optimize recovery. But what makes them unique is that their recovery is rooted in Dislocation Theory. They now have the theoretical tools to help them identify the forces arrayed against them—from economic displacement to Big Pharma to the prison-industrial complex. They have contextualized their experiences; they understand that the opioid epidemic did not occur in a vacuum and that addiction is actually the result of many factors. Unlike earlier generations, they have taken the time and made the effort to do research and educate themselves. Their arsenal is much bigger as a result.

Real progress is being made at the hands of recovered addicts and their allies. Addicts are getting better at scale—literally by the thousands. Yet they are ignored by the media and have been never been invited to help craft policy. Why? Our politicians are supposed to be our elected representatives, yet they act like we don't even exist—or don't matter.

The solution to this crisis isn't going to come from government, doctors, law enforcement, or academics. It's got to come from us—the recovered addicts and our allies addressing what is really going on and not simply following the lead of those who deny that we can ever truly heal or, worse still, seek to profit from our suffering. We will win this war. It may take decades, but with God's help, we will prevail—one addict at a time.

This is our mission.

16

REAL PEOPLE REAL RECOVERY

This battle is just beginning but our tribe is growing. As in every war, there are casualties and in this epic battle against addiction, it is no different. In fact, the casualties are staggering—overdoses, orphaned children, parents burying their kids.

But there are also victories and heroes. Here in this section, you will meet some inspiring people who prove that there is reason to hope—living, breathing examples of people who have not only beaten addiction, but have emerged so with a renewed zeal for life and a deep desire to help others; in other words, *recovered addicts*.

We called this book *Real People Real Recovery*, because we know that there are many thousands of addicts who have survived the very worst and lived to tell about it. At one point, they were hopeless. They were the people our parents warned us against.

We have felt the shame and stigma of addiction. But we also know what it takes to rise above it and feel proud of ourselves. It comes from making amends and serving others. It comes when you realize that you have become an asset to your community.

Eric does street outreach in some of the roughest neighborhoods of the gritty New Hampshire cities of Manchester, Nashua, and Salem. In December 2018, he went to a notorious park in Manchester to try to help some addicts who were living the life he was living just 12 years earlier. While there, he met a young member of the tribe named Mikey, who had been in recovery for 22 months. Like Eric, Mikey knew that it was vitally important to his own recovery that he work to help those in need.

"I do a lot of reaching out to the homeless community, because I used to be one," he told Eric that afternoon. "I try to share the message and some hope . . . I see a lot of my friends are out there with the meth and stuff. It's getting bad. But I have a purpose in life—and that's to help people," he added. "So that's what I'm working on right now."

Eric is at home on the streets because of his years of active addiction. While he is comfortable speaking in boardrooms and packed auditoriums or testifying before congressional subcommittees, he feels most at home in the trenches, speaking with others just like himself.

"I like being out there," he says. "It's where it all started . . . You have to get out there and do something."

CALVIN'S STORY

One of Eric's favorite success stories involves an old high school classmate named Calvin. Their paths crossed again and again, both while Eric was using and after he got clean. Calvin knows the depths of opiate addiction. At one point, he was homeless and living under a bridge in a rough area of Lawrence, MA—not a safe place to be. He lived a life of crime—breaking into buildings and stealing copper to sell to support his habit. In the winter, living under the bridge on the shore of the icy Merrimack River, his pants would literally freeze.

Calvin grew up in a middle-class family, with stable parents and a brother. He started using in his early teens and by age 16, he was using heroin. He was homeless at 20.

He and a young woman with whom he used drugs ended up having a baby. He spent time in and out of jail, rehabs, and hospitals. He reached out to Eric a few years ago and made his way to Granite Recovery Centers (GRC). He went through detox and a 30-day treatment program before graduating to sober living. He worked the 12 Steps diligently. He made amends to his family, paid off restitution for past crimes, and got a job. His daughter was being raised by the mother's grandparents because he and the mother had been deemed unfit. Today, Calvin is employed full time as a mechanic and has his own apartment. He was recently given full custody of his daughter and is a great dad.

Calvin spends much of his spare time trying to help men who are trying to get clean. He looks like a totally different person than the man who first checked in to GRC. When he arrived, his eyes were dark and gray. He gave off an air of despair and couldn't look anyone in the eye.

Now he's got bright eyes. He looks people in the eye and shakes hands firmly. He's not struggling to stay clean. He doesn't suffer the mental obsession. He's proud to be a man in recovery. He shows up to work every day and is a supportive and reliable presence in the lives of his family, friends, and sponsees. His life makes sense.

We have seen this type of transformation over and over again. But we have also attended too many funerals to count. We've comforted more grieving family members than we care to remember. But we are also seeing more and more people find real recovery.

In this day and age, recovery as a word has been watered down like a cheap bumper sticker. But there's a realness to it, it is nothing if not hard-earned. And for those of us who have done the work to attain it, it is invaluable. It's a transformation that occurs from the inside out.

The difference between being sober and being recovered is that with mere sobriety, we are still suffering from being restless, irritable, and discontent (RID) and dealing with the mental obsession. One of the big downfalls of the treatment industry is the lack of shared terminology. Furthermore, there is too much focus on addictive behavior and not enough on the real problem, which is the internal condition of the addict. We are told that sobriety is the solution. Or that medication-assisted treatment is the answer. But the reality is, in both cases, we are still suffering and vulnerable.

Addiction is a condition of the mind, the body, and the emotions. If we are sober, but haven't addressed the internal condition, we are still in pain. We are still depressed, bored, lonely, irritable, and angry. We can't stand to be in our own skin, and we are plagued with thoughts of using.

To be recovered is to be abstinent and obsession free. The steps treat the underlying emotional condition. When people recover, something clicks. It's a magical process but it is also very practical—the addict follows a specific set of directions in order to achieve a particular goal. It is something that can be easily replicated by others. There is no guesswork to it. It is a matter of doing the work with integrity.

We often use the analogy of fitness. You may have all the information you need on how to get into shape—knowing what to eat, how to work out, which exercises to do, how many reps, the proper form, when to rest, etc. But if you don't execute—if you don't actually do it—it has no actual value to your real life.

It's the same with recovery. If you are earnest and honest and have good guidance, you will get results. Then it is only a matter of elbow grease. Do the work and get better. Sooner or later, it clicks. It definitely clicked for the following folks.

CAROLYN'S STORY

Carolyn Murphy is the daughter of an affluent couple from central Massachusetts. She started drinking and experimenting with drugs at a very young age. By the time she was 18, she was an active alcoholic and had a serious cocaine and crack habit. Somehow, she managed to graduate high school. However, when she went off to college her drug and alcohol abuse exploded. She lived in a constant state of chaos—benders, blackouts, and shame.

She flunked out of college and moved home where she began running the streets of Fitchburg, a tough mill town about 45 minutes west of Boston. She jumped from relationship to relationship and began using heroin at age 21. She overdosed and went to detox seven different times.

She couldn't get clean and she didn't know why. Shooting heroin wasn't enough, so she started mixing dope with sedatives like Xanax, Klonopin, and other benzodiazepines. Her last two years of using are a complete blank. She was in a near perpetual blackout. She lied and stole. She scammed her family and friends for money, leading many of them to cut her out of their lives. She descended into prostitution.

Her mother cut off all contact but her dad still tried to help her, despite the depths she had fallen to. "I was still his baby girl," she recalls.

For many years Carolyn had sought help through psychiatry. She was first prescribed Prozac at 14 for suicidal ideation. When that didn't work, she tried virtually every other selective serotonin reuptake inhibitor (SSRI), such as Zoloft, Celexa, and Lexapro.

From 13 to 18 she was prescribed Adderall. Needless to say this only fueled her addiction further. She continued filling her script after she turned 18, but by then was only using it as a party drug and as something to barter for coke.

Toward the end of her using, she was prescribed powerful neuroleptic medications like Thorazine and Seroquel. Carolyn says, "I was a walking zombie. My tongue stuck to the roof of my mouth. I could think thoughts but couldn't communicate them. Once, I had to use hand signs to try to explain to the director of a treatment center that I wanted to get off the meds."

Medication did nothing to arrest the cycle of her addiction. She overdosed. Her kidneys failed. She woke up in parking lots with needles in her hands and neck. She was arrested for possession, assault, and numerous driving offenses. Her dad finally retrieved her from a trap house and brought her to a detox in southeastern Massachusetts.

She was hallucinating. She left the program and tried to jump off of the Tobin Bridge in Boston. Soon after, she overdosed at her parents' house. That's when they were referred to Granite Recovery Centers. Her father drove her to Green Mountain Treatment Center, a sprawling, 72-acre respite tucked into the scenic landscape of northern New Hampshire.

The staff at Green Mountain explained to her what it meant to be a drug addict. They introduced her to the model of addiction. It explained what she was suffering from in a way that nothing else had. What she learned made sense. She bought in to the program.

"These people understand what I'm feeling. They seem to get it," she told herself. "And they seem better than okay—they seem to be enjoying their lives."

She started working the 12 Steps. She discharged from GRC at step six and moved into a sober-living facility. But her addiction was relentless. She relapsed and overdosed. She went to another GRC facility, New

Freedom Academy, and tried all over again. There she learned even more about addiction and Dislocation Theory.

"I had to change a lot of ideas and who I was," she says. "I was still living in a frame of mind that no longer served me."

Carolyn learned that what was missing in her life was connection. One of the key tenets of both Dislocation Theory and recovery is that the opposite of addiction isn't sobriety—it is connection.

"I had never really understood that, but when it was explained to me it finally made sense," she remembers. "I couldn't connect to other people; at least not until I met all these women who were battling these same things day in and day out. It was an unconditional love from people who understood. I had unconditional love from my family but they didn't understand the way I thought or why I did things."

She finally surrendered. Things began to move in a dramatically different direction. "I got vulnerable and that brought me to the connection I was longing for my whole life," Carolyn says. "Everyone on this planet just wants to feel love. It can be from an animal, a significant other, anything. That's what we all crave. It's human nature. For a drug addict running the streets, to say I need help and I need the connection—that's what gets you well. It comes with a lot of hard work to surrender to that belief system. It's the sense of humility. It's self-discovery and connection. At least that's what it boiled down to for me."

Today, Carolyn is 32 and works as an operations supervisor for GRC at New Freedom Academy. Every day she helps women who are just like she was, each struggling to find their path to recovery.

She is completely medication free. She says, "I knew I didn't need the meds. I never should have been put on them in the first place. But once you are on them, they can be hard to get off." Carolyn has come to understand that real recovery is ultimately about meaningful connection and spiritual practice.

"It's beautiful. I have my own apartment, a boyfriend. My family is back in my life," she said. "And beyond my job, I do a lot within the recovery community."

She goes to AA meetings. She has sponsees. She speaks with family members who have loved ones with addiction issues. She picks up *green beans*—newly sober addicts—and brings them to meetings. She volunteers frequently, traveling around Massachusetts and New England to spread the message of recovery and seek out others to help.

"It gets me out of myself," she says. "The root of my drug addiction is selfishness. There are people out there who don't know that there is a solution. When I was out there running, if you had told me that the *Big Book* and this place would help me, I would have told you that you were out of your mind. I feel like it's my privilege to give that to other people and let them know there's a way out. I feel a purpose in my life now. I feel a change."

Most of all, she understands that she's part of this new tribe—a tribe that is taking addiction out of the shadows and bringing the message to the masses.

"I say to my clients a lot or the girls I meet at meetings, welcome to the family. It's more than a bunch of drug addicts and alcoholics, it's really a family. It's bigger than us," she said. "AA used to be a bunch of old guys in a basement smoking butts. Now it's a bunch of 22-year-olds saying, let's have fun in sobriety. You're not alone anymore."

JOHN'S STORY

John Sweek is a 55-year-old businessman in long-term recovery from opiates and alcohol. He started abusing drugs—marijuana and alcohol— as a 15-year-old growing up in Portland, OR. By the time he was 17, he and a friend were forging prescriptions for opioids and other drugs (his friend's father was a doctor). At 19, he injected heroin for the first time.

Unlike the vast majority of opiate addicts, John managed to avoid getting a full-blown heroin habit. He came perilously close numerous times but always managed to pull himself back from the brink. Alcohol was his fall-back drug. He always drank heavily between heroin runs. When his wife confronted him about his drinking, he shrugged it off. John says he thought of drinking as "the cost of doing business—my way of finding relief."

John's ability to avoid becoming a full-blown heroin addict was a function of several factors. His brother and several of his friends had already fallen prey to the needle and he did not want to follow suit. He also moved to Idaho in 1989 and it was hard to score dope. So he fell into a pattern where he would go to Portland on business several times a year, get high, and return home with a small piece of black tar heroin.

His use followed that pattern for the better part of a decade. By 1997, he owned two restaurants and a painting company. He employed as many as 150 people at any given time. John was, by any measure, a high-functioning addict.

Everything came to a head on a cold morning in March 1997. He had gotten drunk at a fundraiser the night before. He still had a small ball of heroin. His plan was to get up early, get high, and then make breakfast for his two children, then 4 and 6 years old. But it wasn't meant to be. Instead, he overdosed and was discovered by his kids lying on the bathroom floor.

He was rushed to the hospital. Initially, the doctors didn't know what was wrong with him. It was only after the syringe (he was still clutching it in his hand) caught on the sleeve of his sweater that they realized that they were dealing with a heroin overdose. They gave him a dose of Narcan. He came to to the sound of his wife screaming, "You motherfucker!"

It was a rude awakening. His denial shattered like a pane of glass. John remembers: "It was a realization with three branches. I knew that I had a problem, that I needed help but didn't know how to get it, and that I was not going home."

John flew (in his pajamas) to Seattle that same day and was admitted to a 28-day residential treatment program. He was lucky. An old friend who had gone through the steps the year before said he'd be happy to sponsor him and take him though the work. Step work was not part of John's treatment, so he spent all his visiting hours going through the *Big Book* with his sponsor. By the time he was discharged, he had completed his fourth step and was ready to read.

He says that he had a major epiphany at the very beginning of the *Big Book*, while still in the *Doctor's Opinion*. He remembers, "Something profound happened when I learned about RID and the alcoholic's inability 'to distinguish the true from the false.' I saw the truth at once. And from that moment I have never been tempted to get high or suffered the mental obsession."

John was served divorce papers while he was still in treatment. His wife also sent him a box—a very large box—packed with his belongings. "I really got the picture when I saw that she had packed the large pepper grinder." Most difficult of all was the specter of not seeing his children. For three months, he could only speak to them on the phone twice a week. "Talking to a 4-year-old on the phone, that's hard."

After leaving treatment, he read his fifth step and moved quickly into the amends process. The amend he made to his wife was particularly hard. John was not allowed to visit or call the house. All communication would be through a mediator. If he called or showed up, she would call the police and obtain a protection from abuse order. She was pissed and she was serious.

In hindsight, John can see that her boundaries were absolutely vital to his recovery. It gave him no choice but to put his recovery first. He says, "No promise, no carrot, and absolutely no contact. That's what I needed to get better."

He had a lot on his plate. He was roughly $200,000 dollars in debt and had to manage three businesses and 150 employees. He spoke with his sponsor every day and attended meetings faithfully. At two months he was allowed to co-parent his children. At three months he started sponsoring people himself. And he paid off his debts—every cent.

After a year he told his wife that he either wanted to get back together or to move on. She told him to get his stuff and come home. His wife had worked hard on herself during the time John was away. She knew that it was no accident that she had married him. She had attended Al-Anon but was disturbed by how many people there were trying to learn how to live with a sick person. She quickly realized that she wanted to learn how to live without one.

John is no longer a sick person. He is a recovered addict and a pillar of his community. A devoted husband, John is also the proud father of three beautiful, successful children. He still attends meetings and can say, "I've never gone six months without taking someone through the steps. When someone asks, I always say *yes*."

Piers says that John is "one of the most capable and successful sponsors" he has ever had the pleasure of knowing.

John advises addicts who are coming into recovery to "take the steps early so the doors can open wide." He admires those addicts and alcoholics who are always "growing, taking risks, and learning new things." He believes that real recovery is ultimately about freedom.

JAMES'S STORY

James Ryan is a 42-year-old doctoral candidate in long-term recovery from polysubstance addiction. Compared to the other folks in this chapter, his using career was brief and dramatic.

James started abusing drugs as an 18-year-old. An epic LSD binge landed him in a psychiatric hospital when he was 19. He responded well to the medications (Stelazine and Cogentin) and his psychosis subsided. However, he couldn't handle the side effects. So after being discharged he found a psychiatrist who took him off his meds and prescribed him Klonopin.

For the next year James abused Klonopin and marijuana. He also kept weaving in and out of psychosis. He remembers, "I could interpret traffic and became convinced that my parents were trying to kill me."

Eventually, his family sent him to rehab in Arizona. He was put back on neuroleptics but stopped taking them shortly after his psychosis cleared. However, he soon became depressed and was prescribed Effexor.

From rehab James went to a year-long wilderness-based life skills program for at risk youth in Oregon. It was a good experience. Looking back from the perspective of Dislocation Theory, James could see that life in the community served as a small oasis of integration. He felt so much better that he asked the doctor to taper him off the Effexor. However, he suffered strange *brain zaps* for an extended period of time.

James struggled after he left the wilderness program. He held a few jobs and went through an ugly relationship break up. He no longer had a sense of community or purpose. Once again, he found himself sinking into a dark depression.

In 2002, he enrolled at Northland College in Wisconsin. He wanted to study wilderness therapy so he could work in the field. Once again, he found himself relatively happy and depression free. He had friends and a sense of purpose. It all came to an end, however, when he went through another painful breakup.

He decided to transfer to the University of Maine in Farmington. Unfortunately, it only made matters worse. He was alone in a strange town, working part-time at a bottle redemption center. Much to his horror, he started having psychotic symptoms again. "I could hear things scratching outside my window (which was on the second floor) and I knew people were out to get me." Desperate, he started attending NA meetings. Shortly thereafter, he met a guy who suggested that he attend the local *Big Book* meeting.

James was frightened and intrigued by what he saw and heard. He could see that these folks were doing well but he was terrified at the idea of "seeking guidance from God." He had had his fill of voices in his head. Plus, his dad was a minister and he felt that he had rejected the God business long ago.

But he was interested and really did not want to continue on the path he was on. So with some trepidation he took up the work. He was particularly agitated on the day of his third step. As he went to meet his sponsor to say the prayer, a voice in his head started repeating, "Thy will, not mine be done"—again and again. But the voice wasn't alien or frightening. James says, "It wasn't attacking me. It was from me, but it was not me—if that makes any sense."

His fourth step was a series of epiphanies. He invited the Spirit to help write his inventory. James said, "I would pray and the answers would come. It was like my own heart was telling me a secret." Reading his fifth step was dramatic as well. "Steps five through seven revealed another person. Someone new, yet someone I could clearly recognize."

James knew he had changed when he went to the *Big Book* meeting a few days after he had read his inventory. "Two women were talking in the parking lot outside the meeting. I walked up to them and chatted briefly before I went inside. There was no social anxiety. I was open and attentive, not worried about what others were thinking about me." James was living out the promise that the steps would afford him "freedom from the bondage of self."

James's most powerful amends happened at the funeral of his friend, George. James made the amends after the congregation was asked if anyone would like to share a few words. While speaking, James couldn't stop asking himself, "Why him and not me?" It was then that he realized that the closest he would ever get to answering that question would be through the practice of the twelfth step. He says, "Maybe I can do something for someone else. It is the only thing that makes sense."

James is recovered and medication free. He is happily married and the father of two very bright and talented children. He has not had any psychotic symptoms since he commenced down this path all those years ago. He has sponsored many men and even worked in the field for over a year. However, his real passion is research. A naturally curious person, he was puzzled why so few people did the steps. And how is it that they still even exist? What is the real history of AA and the Oxford Group?

James is working on a dissertation that explores how addicts and alcoholics use writing in recovery. He is learning many new things that are, in turn, giving him new ideas about how to deepen and expand his own approach to step work. In academic terms, James sees himself as making an *intervention in the field*. He wants to offer something unique, something valuable to others who are seeking recovery.

We believe that he has already succeeded. James is one of the best researchers in the world of 12-Step recovery. If you want to get a sense of the depth and quality of his work, please visit his website at www.stepstudy.org.

RANDY'S STORY

Randy Smith (not his real name) is 41 years old and in recovery from opioid addiction. Raised on the North Shore of Massachusetts, he was a standout three-sport (football, baseball, and basketball) athlete in high school. Piers describes him as "the most severely addicted" opiate addict he has ever known.

Like many of our clients, Randy did not become addicted until he was exposed to opioids as a college freshman in 1996. Prior to that, he was a typical high school kid, smoking a little pot and drinking on weekends.

Initially, he only abused Percocet and Vicodin here and there. He caught a habit in 1999 after he began abusing 40 mg OxyContin (OC 40s). Before long, he dropped out of school and began dealing full time.

In January of 2002 he moved to Palm Beach County, FL. At the time, there were less than 15 pain management clinics operating in the area. "Patients" still had to be cautious about doctor shopping. But even in 2002, Randy was getting prescriptions filled at three to five different clinics. Each doctor would prescribe him roughly sixty OC 40s for about $300. All transactions were made in cash. He also was able to get 60 Oxycodone 30s for "breakthrough pain." He filled his scripts every 28 days, paying $150 per visit.

From the start, he moved the drugs to Massachusetts to sell at a substantial markup. Randy was but one of many thousands of entrepreneurial dealers who would take full advantage of the pill mills of south Florida. He says, "I played the game and worked my way up."

Randy worked the pill mill angle for roughly a decade, from 2002 to 2012. As business ramped up and pain management clinics opened on every street corner, all pretense toward legitimacy went out the window. Randy recalls, "At first, they tried to look legit. You had to show evidence of injury. Before long it got so that any 18-year-old could go into a clinic and get prescribed 180 Oxycodone 30s. All he had to do was buy a fake MRI."

By 2003, Randy was getting 120 OC 80s, 240 Oxycodone 30s, two bottles of liquid OxyContin (equivalent to 7.5 80-mg pills), and 120 2-mg Xanax, from a single doctor. Meanwhile, his own habit had gone through the roof. He recalls how he would begin his day by taking 10 to 15 Oxyco-done 30s and drinking half a bottle of liquid Oxycontin.

Business flourished. Addicts came from all over the eastern United States to get their prescriptions filled. Dealers grew increasingly brazen and innovative. Randy reports that he would sponsor up to 10 people at a time to get prescriptions filled for him. This means Randy would pay for his *sponsee's* bogus MRI, doctor's visit, and prescription for a cut of the drugs. At one point, he even employed a grandmother. He also always had several dealers working for him in Massachusetts.

The Oxy era ended around 2011, largely as a result of bad press. But new regulations and stiffer enforcement did not spell the end of the pain management clinics. They simply marketed different drugs, moving from OxyContin to methadone to Oxycodone and Dilaudid.

Despite his involvement in the drug trade, Randy sought help again and again. He estimates that he has been to detox and/or residential treat-ment between 50 and 75 times. He was also in several methadone pro-grams. He reports, "I was up to 140 mg of methadone a day, but that doesn't include what I was getting from the doctor."

Randy was also witness to the massive expansion of the treatment in-dustry in south Florida. "It was a fucking joke. All about the money. No different than the pill mill game. In fact, some of the very same play-ers who had opened pain management clinics opened treatment centers. Now Delray is known as the *recovery ghetto* of the United States."

Randy finally found recovery a year ago. His detox was long and har-rowing; he was still suffering symptoms of post-acute withdrawal eight months into sobriety. To say that he is relieved and grateful to be in recov-ery would be a massive understatement. He says he owes his recovery to the *Big Book* and the 12 Steps, yoga, research, and knowledge.

Of the steps he says, "I cried the first time I heard that you could be recovered. The *Big Book* explained what was wrong with me. Before that, I thought that I was just really screwed up. I needed help from someone who really cared and knew what it was like to have RID and the mental obsession."

Randy believes that yoga is the best thing for an addict's body. He says, "We are cut off from our physical selves. Now it is like my body talks to me."

He also follows the White Bison program, which is a Native American 12-step movement. It has taught Randy about the role that intergenerational trauma plays in addiction and how the suffering of our ancestors impacts the present generation. White Bison has also taught him the importance of making a spiritual connection to the Earth. Don Coyhis, the founder of White Bison, stresses that addiction only takes hold in cultures that are cut off from the natural world.

Randy has also dedicated himself to studying the game. He is a student of the work of Robert Whitaker, Sam Quinones, Bruce Alexander, and others. "Research has shown me how the system is rigged against you. They need people to stay sick because a sick patient is a profitable patient. Just putting people in a druggy buggy and carting them from meeting to meeting and giving them psych meds is not the same as actually caring for the addict. Treatment has become babysitting and warehousing people, just like the prison-industrial complex. And some people are getting filthy stinking rich while people's kids and parents are dying."

As of this writing, Randy is the manager of a sober living house and has several sponsees.

ALEX'S STORY

Another reality of the current opioid epidemic is that it is taking down tens of thousands of very young people. When the *Big Book* was written, the prototypical alcoholic was a middle-aged white man in his 40s or 50s. For many alcoholics, it took a long, long time to find their way to those church basements. Today, it is not uncommon to walk into a meeting and see a sea of very young women and men—young women like Alex Lincoln.

Like Carolyn, Alex grew up in a very stable, supportive family. But by 21, her life had spiraled completely out of control. She was on the verge of death at an age when many people are looking toward graduating from college and entering the job market.

When she was in high school, she blacked out behind the wheel and was arrested for driving under the influence. Her parents helped her get a lawyer and got her into rehab. But this was just the beginning of a long, dark descent.

She continued drinking heavily and began taking pills—Xanax, Klonopin, and other benzos. She worked in restaurants and drank heavily with her coworkers after work. She started using cocaine. She also had a friend who was abusing heroin; it wasn't long before Alex was doing it with her. Soon, she was making regular trips from New Hampshire to Lawrence, MA to score dope.

"It was off to the races," she says. "I understood the seriousness of it, but I thought I was invincible. I felt untouchable."

Like Carolyn, Alex was prescribed a gamut of psychiatric medications for roughly a decade. She was first prescribed SSRIs in middle school. Later, she would be given Lithium and Effexor. And like Carolyn, she would eventually be prescribed powerful neuroleptics (i.e., Abilify and Latuda). Alex said that these drugs gave her a constant dry mouth and rendered her *numb and zombie-like*. They didn't slow her using at all.

Her family sent her to rehab in Michigan. She went through a 30-day program and decided to move to California to try sober living with some other people from the treatment center. She landed in a sober house in Los Angeles. It couldn't have been a worse place.

She started drinking again and one day, she just took off. She had no family and no real friends in California. She couch surfed and slept in cars and on the streets. She lost all contact with her family.

But her dad never gave up; he took a trip out to L.A. to find her. Somehow, he managed to track her down. When he found her, she looked like she had climbed out of a gutter. She hadn't brushed her hair in weeks and was covered in dirt. He got her into another treatment center in Florida, but again, it wasn't the place for her.

As Randy stated earlier, the treatment industry in Florida is rife with hustlers and scam artists who prey on addicts and their families. Alex was shuffled from one facility to another until she just gave up and left treatment yet again. Before long she was doing crystal meth.

She moved back to Massachusetts and wound up living with another addict who was mentally ill and extremely violent. She had an epiphany while living there, thinking: "What the hell am I doing? I'm going to die."

Her dad picked her up at the trailer park where she was staying and brought her to New Freedom Academy where she got sober and began her journey to recovery. After going through the program there, she went on to sober living.

"I think the main difference was that I had to do the work," she explains of what changed for her when she got to New Freedom Academy. "I had to actually put in an effort to change. At all the other facilities, it was just kind of hang out in your pajamas all day and do whatever you want. Those other centers would take us to 12-Step meetings but they never told us to get a sponsor or actually do the 12 Steps. GRC pushed me a lot. They held me accountable, which I had not been—ever," she adds. "They told me I was selfish and self-centered and that I had a part in what had happened to me. It was freeing almost because it forced me to take responsibility."

Like Carolyn, Alex now sponsors several other women. She's made amends to her family, friends, and many of the businesses she either worked for or stole from, or both. It's been an emotional roller coaster but she's got two years of recovery and is excited about her future—one which just a few years ago she didn't believe she would ever have.

Alex is also medication free. She came off all of her medications when she was about six months into recovery. Coming off Effexor was especially hard. "I had brain zaps and my head and vision were shaky. When I first came off the meds I was super moody and emotional. But it wasn't long before I started feeling good—now I feel better than I have ever felt in my whole life." Today, Alex is inspired to help others.

"Every day I'm fortunate to be able to spread this message," she said. "Me and my family are closer than we've ever been. The relationships that I've formed since being clean are the most amazing relationships ever."

JOE'S STORY

Joe Curran, 30, was another early starter. Joe grew up north of Boston in the wealthy suburb of Hamilton, MA. His parents didn't get married until he was 19 and he grew up living with his grandparents. His parents lived close by and he says he had a mostly normal and happy childhood. That all changed when he was just 11 and he tried drinking for the first time.

He was with a friend and they tried Kahlua and gin. The youngsters preferred the Kahlua because they thought it tasted like chocolate. Joe doesn't remember much from that first experience, except that he got drunk and that he felt like he had found something that he liked—very much.

"I got a lot of relief from it," he says. "It made me feel good for sure."

Joe said his experience that first time was much like the story told in the *Big Book* by Bill Wilson when he says that the first time he drank "the whole face of the universe instantly changed" for him.

"That happened to me. I very much had that same reaction," Joe says. "It made me feel so good."

Joe added: "I don't think I realized how much pain I was in until I tried drinking for the first time. The pain was normal. It was nothing new. Once I got the relief, I told myself 'I want to feel like this.'"

The next year, he tried weed. By age 15, he was a regular drinker. "I don't think I was an alcoholic from the first time I drank, but the wheels were in motion at that point," he says. "I definitely thought about more ways to drink."

During his sophomore year of high school, he tried cocaine and began using it regularly, often to extend and/or enhance his drinking binges. In 2007, he went to college in Boca Raton, FL. It was the heyday of the pill mill boom and soon Joe was right in the thick of the exploding opioid frenzy.

A guy across the hall from him in his residence hall sold Xanax and Percocet 30s. Called *Roxies*, Joe could buy them for just $8 each. Two mg *zanny bars*—Xanax pills—were just $1.

"The amount of pills going around at that time was mind-boggling," he remembers. "I sniffed Xanax all the time. When I sniffed the Xanax, I didn't need to drink as much. If I had $7, I could get 14 mg of Xanax. That was plenty."

He started skipping classes and not surprisingly, his grades suffered. It came to a point where he either had to drop out or he would flunk out, so he quit school and moved back to Massachusetts.

Back in Massachusetts, the pill frenzy was in full swing. His friend was hooked on OxyContin and Joe asked him if he could get the Roxies. The friend told him he couldn't, but what he could get was heroin.

"He told me he could get brown—I didn't know what he meant. Then he said 'H'—I still didn't know what he was talking about," Joe recalls. "Eventually I figured it out. I said 'Oh no, I'm good.' But then the wheels started to spin in my head."

He called the friend back and soon he found himself on his first car ride to nearby Lynn, MA to score heroin.

"That car ride changed the course of my life," he says.

He sniffed it at first.

"It was euphoric. I loved it," he said. "It definitely took away all the stress."

He was a pretty classic alcoholic and drank regularly. But once he was introduced to heroin, he stopped drinking altogether and focused solely on the powerful narcotic. He was instantly hooked.

Within a day or two, he couldn't get heroin, so he tried Suboxone for the first time. He hadn't yet developed an opiate habit and the Suboxone got him *jammed*—or high. Suboxone, as previously discussed, isn't designed to have intoxicating effects but a new user can get very high by taking it, while experienced addicts can easily take enough to get high. Joe crushed up a pill and sniffed it. He got very sick, but also very high.

Soon, he was buying heroin daily. He was living with his parents and they started catching on to his addiction, so he moved out. He went to live with a girl he was friends with who was also an addict. She eventually lost her job and car and they couldn't afford the apartment they were in, so they went to live at her mother's house.

For about a year, the two lived there, using regularly. After Joe stole her mother's debit card and a bottle of Xanax, he was kicked out of the house. He found himself homeless for the first time. He went back to his parents and asked for help and was sent to a Suboxone clinic.

He went through withdrawals at the clinic and was given small increments of Suboxone to curb the symptoms. He was prescribed 16 mg Suboxone pills and was required to take regular drug tests. He also met regularly with a clinician who educated him about potential liver problems linked to opioid abuse.

He laughed when he was told that Suboxone would block the cravings but not get him high. He knew that it was common for addicts to take enough to *break through* so they could, in fact, get high. He also says he once saw another addict shoot their Suboxone and overdose.

He continued his regular sessions but soon started shooting cocaine. He kept failing his drug tests and wound up in the hospital after mixing Suboxone and intravenous cocaine. He was kicked off the Suboxone program and turned to shooting heroin.

He was also on antidepressants and found himself in a cycle of failed detox and recovery attempts. He went back to a different Suboxone clinic. He went to an in-patient rehab in Massachusetts and then to a treatment center in New Hampshire. There, he kicked his Suboxone habit but with a near-fatal caveat: he didn't sleep for 13 days.

His eyes watered, his nose ran, and he was sneezing. It was October and he wore two pairs of sweatpants and two sweatshirts to stave off the chills. He laid in bed all day in an agonizingly uncomfortable state.

He left that treatment center and immediately went to score heroin. He went on a run and slept in his girlfriend's car for three weeks. Over the next year, he would go in and out of roughly 20 different treatment centers, each time failing to find recovery. "I didn't want to be better," he said. "The only reason I was going in and out of treatment was because I was homeless."

Suicide started to become an option. Once those thoughts started, he realized internally that something had to change. "That's when I really wanted to be better," he said.

Still, despite his desire to find recovery, he failed repeatedly. He went through 10 centers. "That's when it really started to get scary for me," he said. "Now I wanted to be better, but I was still getting high and didn't have an excuse. I was powerless."

He landed at a sober house in Malden, MA where there were no drug testing or breathalyzer policies. He remained sober for four months before he relapsed. He didn't shower, didn't sleep, and was sick constantly.

He went back on Suboxone, mainly, he says, as a crutch so that he wouldn't get sick if he couldn't score heroin or cocaine.

It was a call from a friend who had recently gotten clean that pushed him to try detox again. He went to a facility in Maine, surrendered, and started doing the 12 Steps. He went through the steps very quickly and made it to Step 12 in a month and a half.

"I had accepted that I was totally powerless at that point," he remembers. "I just really, truly wanted to get sober. Before that, I just needed somewhere to go or wanted to get someone off my back."

That was in February 2011, and Joe has been recovered ever since. He's now the 12-Step Director at Granite Recovery Centers' New Freedom Academy. He lives in New Hampshire with his wife, who is also recovered, and they have three children.

"The biggest thing that's different for me is I don't ever fight with thoughts of using," he said. "I would consider myself to be a recovered addict. I'm relatively content most of the time. I have a house, I have a car, I own things, I have a job. I'm content. I can show up for my family. I can try and help other people."

It's the helping part that he says is crucial to his recovery. "Just getting to watch someone and watch them grow up in recovery and turn around and help someone else. That's amazing," he said. "There are way more failures than success stories, but once in a while you really get to see someone who gets well and they go back to their lives and become family men and women and there's something special about that."

SUMMARY

These are the remarkable stories of some very remarkable people. Several important themes run throughout their narratives:

- All of them healed through the 12 Steps. They are all medication free and no longer suffer the mental obsession.
- They found recovery only after having reached a depth of suffering and despair.

- They are energized to help others.
- They are all deeply curious and want to learn and do more.

The reader may object that these stories are exceptional and that one cannot expect this kind of success from every addict who takes the steps. We agree—up to a point. First of all, the fact that many addicts do not get better in the steps is no reason to stop trying. Also, we know of no comparable modality—nothing that can consistently deliver the quality of recovery described in the previous stories. And finally, recovered addicts are numerically significant. There are thousands upon thousands of such stories.

We believe there could be many more if we carried the message far beyond the confines of the various fellowships. Rates of recovery could be further enhanced if we deliberately integrated the steps into a well-rounded holistic treatment modality informed by Dislocation Theory.

The overdose statistics we see in the news are (no pun intended) sobering—they are horrible, in fact. But hope exists. Real recovery exists. Eric and Piers see it everywhere, in themselves and in others. People like Calvin, Carolyn, John, James, Randy, Alex, and Joe are living it each and every day.

"Every time someone gets better, a battle is won," Eric says. "Growing the tribe is winning. Every person who finds recovery has the power to affect hundreds of others in a positive way."

And that's how this war will be won: *one success at a time.*

17

CONCLUSION

This book raises some awkward and controversial issues. It critiques virtually all the major institutions that a person typically identifies with the worlds of addiction and recovery, especially the 12-Step movement, professional psychology, and the pharmaceutical industry. As a society, we are deeply ambivalent and conflicted about what addiction actually is, what it tells us about ourselves, and how it should be treated. Is it actually a *disease*? Should addicts be punished? Is real recovery even feasible for a majority of addicts?

THE SPIRITUAL QUESTION

This book raises an even deeper question about the relationship between spirituality and psychology—about what it means to be human. Are we merely biological creatures? Does biochemistry provide the best model for understanding human suffering? There are many schools of psychology (e.g., transpersonal, Jungian, Buddhist, pastoral) that maintain that spirituality is essential to human well-being—that meaning and fulfillment cannot be achieved through worldly pursuits or the mere accumulation of wealth. These perspectives have been marginalized by academia and the treatment world because they are explicitly spiritual and thereby constitute a threat to the dominant paradigm of biological psychiatry.

The 12 Steps are a *living* spiritual stream. They have been practiced by millions of people from around the world for over 80 years. New members are initiated into the ranks on a daily basis. They are eminently practical—they are an effective spiritual *medicine* for one of the great maladies of our time. They are a set of exercises that bring one from crisis to conversion and, ultimately, to a mystical experience.

Where the steps draw their power from the spiritual, professional psychology has adopted the premises of biological psychiatry. Treatment centers acknowledge the value of AA or NA but most centers never seriously consider the efficacy of the 12 Steps. The fact that treatment centers cannot even be licensed or receive third-party reimbursement without the presence of a staff psychiatrist shows just how marginal spirituality is to the overall system.

The reader may object that treatment centers should not be in the business of *religion*, even if it is of the non-denominational, 12-Step variety. We agree that no one should be forced to take up a spiritual practice, but the 12 Steps should be given their due and be acknowledged as a viable (and often very successful) treatment modality. However, this is not likely to happen. Instead, the federal government has released over a billion taxpayer dollars to help subsidize medication-assisted treatment (MAT). We believe that abstinence-based treatment should receive comparable support. It should ultimately be a matter of client choice. Clients should be able to access the services they want. That being said, we have almost no expectation that the situation will change. Big Pharma is one of the most powerful lobbies in the country. Recovered addicts have no comparable clout.

But we do have other options. We have one another and many good friends in high places. We have social media. We have our voices. We have the tribe.

We hope this book will inspire thousands of recovered addicts and alcoholics to step forward and share their experiences with the world at large. We do not intend to cause conflict around the 12 Traditions. We respect the legacy of AA and are committed to its mission. We simply believe that in order for us to address the current addiction crisis, we need to morph and evolve.

We beg our readers to consider that maybe we are being deliberately ignored because what we are saying does not support or validate the assumptions of the system. Addicts are dying in unprecedented numbers and the mortality rate is only going up. Being recovered—free of the mental obsession and all addictive substances—is the best outcome an addict can hope for. We know that many more addicts—hundreds of thousands—could recover if we spread the message beyond the confines of *Big Book* meetings and workshops. Big Pharma and many others that are profiting from addiction are only too happy that the recovery movement is anonymous and largely confined to basement meetings. They fear we will mobilize. But we say, "It is time!"

We also realize that many people will take exception to our belief that the 12 Steps are the preeminent treatment modality. We are not trying to offend. We readily concede that the 12 Steps are not the only way an addict can get recovered. Religion has an impressive track record as well. But we have discovered that many of our critics have never actually practiced the steps or ever met a recovered opiate addict. We do not want to sit in judgment of others. MAT should be an easily accessible harm-reduction option. No one should be forced to do anything. We are simply relating our experience and making the argument that many more addicts could recover if they were given the opportunity that was presented to us. Is it possible that you may be passing judgment on something that you have never actually encountered or experienced?

THE POWER OF DISLOCATION THEORY

The main purpose of this book is to show how we have aligned the steps with the Dislocation Theory of Addiction. This combination has enormous potential. We believe that it is already taking our understanding of addiction and recovery to a new level. Dislocation Theory explains:

- The etiology of addiction
- The imperative to address the stress response
- The context of the present epidemic

The etiology, or cause of addiction, has long been debated. Alexander shows that addiction is not a hazard of being human but only occurs under specific social conditions. If we understand those conditions, then we can address the root cause of the problem. According to Alexander, addiction is an adaptive response to sustained psycho-social dislocation. In other words, widespread addiction comes about as a result of the loss of community and shared social values. This is amply evident in the United States today. We are all suffering from the effects of dislocation—and it is getting worse all the time. Because dislocation affects everyone, an addict is not so different from the parent who cannot get off her cell phone or the accountant who drinks 20 diet sodas a day. Dislocation Theory also points to the solution—connection. Rates of addiction will only subside if we create community anew.

Dislocation Theory reveals just how much we've come to resemble individual rats locked in cages. We feel stressed, fearful, and alone. Our bodies produce unhealthy amounts of adrenaline and cortisol. We are locked into the sympathetic stress response. Many Americans are overworked, underpaid, and deeply fearful of the future. It is even worse for those in active addiction and/or early recovery. Dislocation Theory explains why it is so essential for addicts to learn to regulate the stress response. We do this in the steps by reading inventory and taking up meditation. We also do it by making new interpersonal connections and by healing the relationships we are already in. But we must take it much further. Dislocation Theory provides the rationale for combining the steps with other somatic practices like yoga, tai chi, or qigong. We believe that *12-Step yoga* may one day be widely recognized as the most effective holistic treatment modality for treating addiction.

Dislocation Theory is also a powerful therapeutic tool for working with addicts in treatment or early recovery. We have found that our clients are very energized when given the means to analyze their condition from a socio-cultural perspective. Understanding the role of Big Pharma in the genesis of the opioid epidemic goes a long way toward removing the stigma surrounding addiction. Putting one's addiction on a historical timeline serves a similar purpose. To ponder that there is a powerful, wildly profitable industry feeding off their addiction, and that it is designed to keep them addicted, can be hugely empowering for addicts. It can give them fuel for their own personal battle as they seek to break the cycle of relapse. Knowledge is always power and we believe it is especially so for addicts seeking recovery.

Identifying dislocation with RID brings the steps and Dislocation Theory into meaningful dialogue. We were all born into a dislocated environment. RID comes with the territory. Martin-Baro's notion of societal sin deepens our understanding even further. It allows us to see how many of our leading institutions are actually causing social fragmentation by rewarding the very worst aspects of human nature (e.g., avarice and xenophobia). This is especially evident in the economic policies that have gutted the middle class over the last 25 years.

The U.S. economic landscape radically changed with the passage of NAFTA. Ross Perot was prescient when he quipped that with the passage of NAFTA there would be a "large sucking sound" as American jobs went overseas to take advantage of cheap labor. The opioid epidemic began a few years later—in 1996—with Purdue Pharma's marketing of OxyContin. At the same time, we saw the birth of the prison-industrial complex. By 2000, the United States was incarcerating a higher percentage of its citizens than any country in the world. The 1990s also marked the advent of the digital age. The pace of change began to increase—faster and faster and faster.

Americans were left bemused and disoriented. Wasn't globalization supposed to raise us all up? Wasn't OxyContin alleged to be nonaddictive? What happened to my town? Why is college so expensive? We are only now beginning to understand the changes that have been thrust upon us. It is like we woke up one day in a totally different world; Huxley's *Brave New World* is in many ways a reality. Kafka's portraits of an alienated citizenry that is at the mercy of a faceless government don't seem that far fetched anymore. Many would argue their bleak societal depictions were prophetic. We are living in a dystopia.

We need to thoroughly analyze this situation if we are going to take effective action. The opioid epidemic is merely a symptom of something much larger. If we really come to understand its causes and conditions, we will also have a much better sense of what we need to do to address our collective problems in a global sense. We will see how the opioid epidemic relates to issues like income stratification, racism, and environmental degradation, and realize how it is really about stress and fear and the loss of shared spiritual values.

GROWING THE TRIBE

Our hope is that this book will serve as a summons to our friends and allies here and abroad. First and foremost, we beg our 12-Step brothers and sisters to step up and make their voices heard. But we also want to forge strong alliances with clergy, clinicians, and somatic practitioners. It is time we pooled our knowledge and skills to transform the 12 Steps into a truly holistic modality, one that heals spirit, soul, and *body*.

We must also reach out to first responders, law enforcement, and the incarcerated. We can help each other through mutual support and an honest exchange of information. We need to be a resource for EMTs after they have resuscitated an addict for the fifth time. We must connect with activists from the worlds of mental health and criminal justice reform. They are our natural allies. We need to do a much better job at reaching out to our veterans, many of whom are suffering in isolation. And we must make contact with recovery communities from around the world. We need your help. Please inform us about what you are doing and what is working in your home country and abroad. The tribe must be global, driven by a genuine respect for all. It transcends all racial, gender, or political affiliations. This is a primal movement—a call to reconnect with our fellow human beings.

Please contact us and share your thoughts and ideas. We look forward to hearing from you. Email us at realrecovery@graniterecoverycenters.com.

IMAGES

Eric testifies about the opioid epidemic before the United States Senate in 2015

Eric talks about President Trump's opioid plan on New England Cable News with host Sue O'Connell in 2018

Eric and Piers at the opening of Granite Recovery Centers headquarters in Salem, N.H. in 2018

Eric and social media guru Gary Vaynerchuk in New York City in 2018

(l to r) Former NFL player and Granite Recovery Centers outreach director Jeff Hatch, rapper/actor Slaine (*Gone Baby Gone* and *The Town*), and Eric at the GRC headquarters in 2018

Eric talks opioids and recovery with Boston's Fox affiliate Boston 25 in 2018

Dr. Bruce Alexander with Eric and his partner, Persephanie Lesperance, at the
Pritts Center at GRC headquarters in New Hampshire in 2018

The packed Pritts Center at GRC headquarters in Salem, N.H. in 2018

Piers and Eric with Dr. Bruce Alexander at GRC's Pritts Center in 2018

Eric, his son Gavin, and partner Persephanie Lesperance, who runs the women's programs for Granite Recovery Centers, in New Hampshire

(l to r) New Hampshire Sen. Andy Sanborn, U.S. Sen. Rand Paul (R-Kentucky), and Eric in 2018

Jeff Hatch and Eric record an episode of the "Real People Real Recovery" podcast in 2018 in Salem, N.H.

Piers speaking in Maine in 2018

Green Mountain Treatment Center, the largest facility of Granite Recovery Centers, includes 72 acres nestled into the Green Mountains of New Hampshire

(l to r) Kevin Martin, Jessica Kaniuka, and Piers, who together founded the non-profit prison advocacy group, the Liberation Institute, which trains inmates at the Maine State Prison to be nationally certified yoga instructors

Eric, his son Gavin, and Eric's dad, Stephen, in 2018

BIBLIOGRAPHY

Alcoholics Anonymous World Services, Inc. (1976). *Alcoholics Anonymous: The Story of How Many Thousands of Men and Women have Recovered from Alcoholism* (3rd Ed.). New York, NY: AA World Services, Inc.

Alcoholics Anonymous World Services, Inc. (2001). *Alcoholics Anonymous: The Story of How Many Thousands of Men and Women have Recovered from Alcoholism* (4th Ed.). New York, NY: AA World Services, Inc.

Alexander, B. K. (1990). *Peaceful Measures: Canada's Way out of the 'War on Drugs'*. Toronto: University of Toronto Press.

Alexander, B. K. (2008). *The Globalization of Addiction: A Study in Poverty of the Spirit*. Oxford, U.K.: Oxford University Press.

Alexander, B. K. (2014). The Rise and Fall of the Official View of Addiction. Retrieved November 18, 2018 from http://www.brucekalexander.com/articles-speeches/277-rise-and-fall-of-the-official-view-of-addiction-6.

Alexander, B. K., et al. (1985). "Adult, infant, and animal addiction." In S. Peele (Ed.), *The meaning of addiction: Compulsive experience and its interpretation* (pp. 73–96). Lexington, MA: D.C. Heath.

Alexander, B. K. and C. S. Shelton, (2014). *A History of Psychology in Western Civilization*. Cambridge, U.K.: Cambridge University Press.

Brand, R. (2017). *Recovery: Freedom from our addictions*. New York, NY: Henry Holt.

Editorial Board of the *New York Times*. (2018, April 21). An opioid crisis foretold. Editorial, *New York Times*.

Grillo, I. (2018, November 15). El Chapo puts the drug war on trial. *The New York Times*. Retrieved November 16, 2018 from https://www.nytimes .com/2018/11/15/opinion/el-chapo-trial-drug-war.html.

Hoffman, J. and S. Froemke. (2007). *Addiction: Why Can't They Just Stop?* New York: Rodale, pp. 40–43.

Kuhn, T. S. (1970). *The Structure of Scientific Revolutions* (2nd Ed. enlarged). Chicago, IL: University of Chicago Press.

Miller, R. (1996). *Drug Warriors and Their Prey: From Police Power to Police State*. Westport, CT: Praeger Publishers.

The Nation. (2018, August 10). Look at Drug Abuse from a Medical Perspective: Paiboon. The Nation (Thailand). Retrieved November 19, 2018 from http://www.nationmultimedia.com/detail/national/30351852.

Quinones, S. (2016). *Dreamland: The True Tale of America's Opiate Epidemic*. London, U.K.: Bloomsbury Press; Reprint edition.

Tick, E. (2014). *Warrior's Return: Restoring the Soul After War* (1st Ed.). Louisville, CO: Sounds True.

Trump, President D. J. (2018, March 19). Remarks by President Trump on Combatting the Opioid Crisis. White House, Washington, D.C. Retrieved November 19, 2018 from https://www.whitehouse.gov/briefings -statements/remarks-president-trump-combatting-opioid-crisis/.

Valliant, G. (2008). *Spiritual Evolution: A Scientific Defense of Faith*. New York: Broadway Books.

Zimbardo, P. and N. Coulombe. (2016). *Man Interrupted: Why Young Men Are Struggling & What We Can Do About It*. Newburyport, MA: Conari Press.

Zoja, L. (2000). *Drugs, Addiction, and Initiation: The Modern Search for Ritual*. Einsiedeln, Switzerland: Daimon Verlag.

INDEX

AA. *See* Alcoholics Anonymous (AA)
A$AP Rocky, 102
abstinence, 39
"abstinence kills," 35, 37, 40, 118, 146
access to treatment, 148
activism, innovation and, 135–136
ADD, 95
Adderall, 95
addiction. *See also* Big Pharma;
    recovered addicts
  active, 43, 47
  Batman story of, xi–xvii
  brain and, 39, 65–66
  cardinal symptom, 39
  as chronically relapsing
    condition, 40
  digital, 122–125
  medicalization of, 93, 94–97
  model of, 3, 39, 88
  as pandemic, 90
  paradigm shift, xi–xviii
  recovery. *See* recovery
  socio-economic dimension, 86
  timeline and trends, 69–77
  traditional cultures and, 86–87
  treatment. *See* treatment
*Addiction Rare in Patients Treated
  with Narcotics,* 98

addictive drugs, xi. *See also* drug
  addicts
ADHD, 95, 96
aerobic exercise, 121
affect regulation, 42
Afghanistan, 100
African Americans, 106, 109
  drug abuse among, 107
  imprisonment rate, 107
aftercare, treatment center and, 149
Agricultural Research, 15
alcohol
  brain and, 65–66
  as money maker, 72
Alcoholics Anonymous (AA),
  xvi–xvii, 31–32. *See also*
  Oxford Group
  anonymous fellowships, 36
  foundation/founders, 31, 156–
    157
  MAT and. *See* medication
    assisted treatment (MAT)
  as movement and cult, 56
  self-help, 142
  as "spiritual kindergarten," 153
  12-Step program. *See* 12-Step
    program
  12 Traditions, 33–34

alcoholism, 69–70. *See also*
     addiction
   economy and, 72
   rates of, 71
   World War I (WWI), 71
aletheia, 43
Alexander, Bruce, 23, 37, 80, 155,
     173. *See also* Dislocation
     Theory
Alexander, Jack, 32
Alexander, Michelle, 155
Alex's story, 173–175
alienation, stress and, 81
American Pain Society, 74
American Psychiatric Association
     (APA), 94
amygdala, 66
annihilation of drug addicts, 114
Anslinger, Harry, 72
anti-psychotics, 95
anxiety, 96
APA. *See* American Psychiatric
     Association (APA)
appropriate staff, treatment center,
     142–143
artificial endorphins, 119
asset forfeiture. *See* civil asset
     forfeiture
Asset Forfeiture Fund of Justice
     Department, 108
attachment, brain and, 65–66
Augustine, St, 51, 90
automation, 85
aversion therapy, 72
Avery, Sandra, 112–113

Batman story of addiction, xi–xvii
Benckiser, Reckitt, 146
benzodiazepines, 96

Big Book, xvii. xviii, 19–22, 28,
     31–32, 36, 39, 41–48, 53,
     55–56, 90–91, 118, 137, 141,
     156. *See* 12-Step program
big data, 102
Big Pharma, 35, 93–104
   medicalization of addiction, 93,
     94–97
   pill mills, 99–103
   pseudoaddiction and, 97–99
bootleggers, 71–72
bootlegging industry, 71–72
Bowden, Charles, 155
brain. *See also* mental illnesses
   addiction and, 39, 65–66
   alcohol and, 65–66
   healing, 120–121
   reward circuitry, 39
Brand, Russell, xvii, 155
Buchman, Frank, 31–32
buprenorphine, 74
Bush, George H. W., 105

Califano, Joseph A., Jr., 129
California, 70
Calvin's story, 160–162
Carolyn's story, 162–165
certification, 136
chemical imbalance theory, 93–94
children, 37
   punished for parent's convictions,
     109
   sex trafficking, 110
chronically relapsing condition, 40
chronic relapsers, 117–118
civil asset forfeiture, 108–109
clinical staff and team. *See* staff/
     staffing, treatment center
Clinton, B., 105–106

Clinton, Hillary, 108
cocaine, 74
   crack *vs.* powder, 105–106
Code of Handsome Lake, 69
communal interdependence, 83
community, treatment centers,
   143–144
companies, using inmate labors,
   110–111
Complementary Alternative
   Medicine, 50
compulsion, 39
concentration of drug addicts,
   110–113
The Concerned Citizens Drug
   Study and Education Society,
   xiii
Concerta, 95
concupiscence, 90
confiscation, of drug addicts,
   108–110
confrontational approach, 144
Contra Rebels, 73
Corrections Corporation of
   America (CCA), 110
cosmologies, 87–88
couples counseling, 124–125
Coyhis, Don, 173
crack epidemic, 73, 74
crack *vs.* powder cocaine, 105–106
crime bill, 105
criminal codes, 112
cultural wisdom, xv
culture, xv
Curran, Joe. *See* Joe's story
Customs and Border Protection, 74

Dark Alliance (Webb), 73
Darwin, Charles, 83

demon drug, 85, 86
Department of Agriculture, 15
digital addiction, 122–125
   gaming, 122–123
   pornography, 123
digital culture and dangers, 80–81,
   124
digital devices, 124
digital technology, 36
dipsomania, 70. *See also* alcoholism
Dislocation Theory, xiv, xviii, 23,
   79–92, 143
   economic forces and, 85
   interconnected ideas of, 82
   moral psychology and, 64–65
   power, 183–186
   power of, 89
   as relative condition, 85
   Tick's findings and, 128
   understanding, 82–90
disordered desire, 90
dopamine, 39
Dreamland (Quinones), 99
Drug Addiction Treatment Act, 74,
   147
drug addicts, 105–114. *See also*
   addiction
   annihilation, 114
   concentration, 110–113
   confiscation, 108–110
   identification, 107
   ostracism, 107–108
drug offenses, 105. *See also* drug
   addicts
   African Americans, 106
   sentencing, 105–106
Drugs, Addiction, and Initiation:
   The Modern Search for Ritual
   (Zoja), 126

drug trade, 76, 86
Drug Warriors and Their Prey: From Police Power to Police State (Miller), 106

Earth, 88
economic forces, 85
education, 136
ego deflation at depth, 45
Einstein, Albert, 83
emotional distress, 119–120
emotional well-being, 83
endorphin deficit, 119
epochal social change, 90
Erikson, Erik, 83
eugenics movement, 64

Facebook, 136
failure to thrive, 122
family support, treatment center and, 144–145
fear, 55
fear mongering, 107
Federal Bureau of Narcotics, 72
fentanyl, 13, 22, 74, 101, 102, 114
Fisher, Rick, 154
Florida, 99
forgiveness, 46
four absolutes, 54–55. *See also* Oxford Group
free services, treatment center and, 148–149
free trade, 85
free trade policies, 86

Gates, Daryl, 108
Generation Adderall, 123
German Jews, 106
globalization, 85

The Globalization of Addiction: A Study in Poverty of the Spirit (Alexander), 82
Granite Recovery Centers (GRC), 23, 27, 28–30. *See also* recovered addicts
family orientation, 145
free services, 148–149
quality aftercare, 149
real recovery stories, 159–180
recidivism/relapse numbers, 132
scholarships, 148

Hannan, Michelle, 110
Hansen, Helena, 95
Hao, Le Van, 128
Hardin, John, 129
hardwired for spiritual experience, 65–67
Harrison Act, 70–71, 74, 107, 147
Hart, Carl, 37, 155
Hazard, Rowland, 60
healthcare organizations, 96
heroin, xi, 70, 85
addicts, 100–101
demand, 100, 101
withdrawal symptoms, xi
Hilberg, Raul, 106
Holocaust, 106
honesty, 55
human suffering, medicalization of, 94–97
Huss, Magnus, 69–70
Huxley, Aldous, 66–67
hydrocodone pills, 99
hyperactivity disorder, 95

identification, of drug addicts, 107
indigenous peoples, 86–87

individual selfishness *vs.* societal
    sin, 90–92
individuation, 62, 63
Inebriate Asylum, 70
informed activism, 135
initiation. *See also* recovery
    failed, 127
    recovery and, 125–128
innovation and activism, 135–136
*An Inquiry into the Effects of Ardent
    Spirits upon the Human Body
    and Mind* (Rush), 69
insecurities, 46
Insys Therapeutics, 102
intent to distribute, 112
intimate relationships, 124–125

James, William, 54, 55, 56–59
James' story, 168–170
Japan, 70
Jick, Hershel, 98
Joe's story, 175–179
John's story, 165–168
Joint Commission on Accreditation
    of Healthcare Organizations
    (JCAHO), 74, 96, 98
Jung, C. G., 60–63, 83, 128

Kelly, John, 133
Kendler, Kenneth, 94
Kerry Committee, 73
King, Martin Luther, Jr., 15
knowledge and spirituality, 36
Kuhn, Thomas, xiv–xv

Levine, Bruce, 91
Liberation Psychology, 91
life sentences, 105
Lincoln, Alex. *See* Alex's story

lobotomies, 72
loss of community, 79–80
loss of social intelligence, 122
love, 55
love drug, 66
LSD, 72, 73

Maine, 16–17
maintenance medications, 95
Man, Interrupted (Zimbardo), 122
Marihuana Tax Act of 1937, 72
marijuana, 72, 73
Martin-Baro, Ignacio, 91–92
Maslow, Abraham, 83
MAT. *See* Medication Assisted
    Treatment (MAT)
Mate, Gabor, 37, 155
Medicaid, 99
medicalization of addiction, 93,
    94–97
medicated society, 103
medication assisted treatment
    (MAT), 118, 119–120, 145–
    148, 153
meditation, 47, 120–121
mental health system, 130
mental illnesses, 64
    chemical imbalance theory,
        93–94
    psychiatric medications, 94
mental obsession, 39–40
mercy, 51–52. *See also* piety
"metanoia," 40
methadone, 73, 145
methamphetamine, 70
Mexico, 100
Millennial addicts, 122–125
Miller, Richard, 106, 155
mood stabilizers, 95

moral code, 44
moral psychology, 63–65
mother-child attachment, 66
Murphy, Carolyn. *See* Carolyn's
    story
Murphy, Morgan, 85
mystical thirst, 128
mystics/mystical experiences, 58

NAFTA, 86, 112
naloxone, 74, 145–146
National Employment Law Project,
    109
National Institute of Drug Abuse
    (NIDA), xiv, 147
    effective treatment program
        basis, 130–131
    recommended treatments for
        addiction, 131
National Institute of Psychology in
    Vietnam, 128
National Institutes of Health, 50
Native Americans, 69
neurology, 64
neuroplasticity, 144
neuropsychology, 50
New England Journal of Medicine, 98
New Freedom Academy, 163–164,
    175
New Testament, 40
New York Quakers, 64
Nicholas II, 71
Nixon, R., 85, 105
novelty, 121
nucleus accumbens, 39

Ohio State University, 15
Olympia, 18
online groups, 136

opiate withdrawal, 26, 119
opioid addiction, 70
opioid crisis, 75, 96, 101–102, 130,
    145
opioid epidemic, 4, 29, 30, 35–36,
    74, 81, 126, 129–130, 155,
    185–186. *See also* Big Pharma
opioid maintenance therapy, 145
opioid sales, 99–100
opiophobia, 96
Opium Commissioner, 70
opium production, 100
orthodoxy *vs.* orthopraxis, 59
orthopraxis *vs.* orthodoxy, 59
ostracism, of drug addicts, 107–108
Oxford Group, 59, 134. *See also*
        Alcoholics Anonymous (AA)
    as an evangelical-pietist
        movement, 56
    confession, 55–56
    four absolutes, 54–55
    inventory, 54–55
    meetings, attendance, 32
    prayer and listening, 55–56
    spiritual exercises, 31–32, 54–56
    surrender, 54
    witnessing, 56
oxycodone pills, 99
OxyContin, 74, 77, 100, 101, 171–172
    demand, 98–99
    potential for addiction, 98
    release of, 98
OxyContin Express. *See* Florida

panic disorders, 96
paradigm shift, xi–xviii
paradoxical effect, 95
Parhamovich, Phil, 108–109
peasants, 83–84

permanent relapsers, 118
pharmaceutical industry, 35,
       93–104. *See also* Big Pharma
pharmaceutical opioid addiction, 97
PIC. *See* prison-industrial complex
       (PIC)
piety, 51–52. *See also* mercy
pill mills, 99–103
pink cloud phenomenon, 134
Plato, xiv
plea bargain agreement, 112
podcast, 136
pop psychology, 48
pornography, 123
Porter, Jane, 98
post-traumatic stress disorder
       (PTSD), 127, 128
powder *vs.* crack cocaine, 105–106
"powerless over drugs and alcohol,"
       44
power of recovered addicts/activists,
       154–156
prayer, 45, 47, 55
prayer and listening, 55–56
PRC. *See* Pritts Recovery Center
       (PRC)
prescription drug abuse, 37
"Prescription Opioid Addiction
       Treatment Study," 147
prevenient grace, 51
price deflation, 74
The Principles of Psychology (James),
       57
prison-industrial complex (PIC),
       110–112
Prison Policy Initiative, 114
prison population, 105, 106
prisons, 37
Pritts Recovery Center (PRC), 148

private prisons, 110–111
process addictions, 82
professionalization, 136
pseudoaddiction, 97–99
psychiatric medications, 94
Psychological Medicine, 94
psychosocial integration, 83, 127–
       128
psychotherapy, 124
public speaking, 136
Purdue Pharma, 74, 76, 77, 98, 101,
       185. *See also* Big Pharma
purity, 55

Quinones, Sam, 99, 155, 173

Randy's story, 171–173
rat laboratory, xiii–xiv
Rat Park, xiv, 82
Reagan, R., 105
real recovery stories, 159–180
       Alex's story, 173–175
       Calvin's story, 160–162
       Carolyn's story, 162–165
       James' story, 168–170
       Joe's story, 175–179
       John's story, 165–168
       Randy's story, 171–173
recovered addicts, 35, 125–128
       activism, 135–136
       as asymptomatic, 127
       power, 154–156
       real stories, 159–180
       RID and, 127
       self-care, 135
       tribe. *See* tribe
recovery. *See also* treatment
       initiation and, 125–128
       as inside job, 134

mission, 156–158
outcomes for, 117–118
pink cloud phenomenon, 134
real stories, 159–180
sobriety compared to, 151–152
surrender and, 118
tribe, 151–158
*Recovery: Freedom from Our
    Addictions* (Brand), xvii
Reding, Nick, 155
reefer madness, 72
relapse, 137
resentment, 46
RID (restless, irritable, and
    discontent), 39, 41–42, 127
Ritalin, 95
Robins, Lee, 85
Roosevelt, Theodore, 70
Rothstein, Arnold, 71
Rush, Benjamin, 69
Russia, 71
Russian-Japanese war, 71
Ryan, James. *See* James' story

SAMHSA. *See* Substance Abuse
    and Mental Health Services
    Administration (SAMHSA)
Sardello, Robert, 22, 88
Satcher, David, 94
Saturday Evening Post, 32
scapegoating, 107
School of Spiritual Psychology, 22
seasonal affective disorder, 70
selective serotonin reuptake
    inhibitor (SSRI), 163
self-care, 144
self-disclosure, 46–47
self-help, 142
selfishness, xviii, 42, 90–91
    individual, *vs.* societal sin, 90–92

sentencing guidelines, 105–106
service, 50–51
sex trafficking, 110
Shadel Sanatorium, 72
shadow complex, 45, 61
Shoemaker, Samuel Moor, 57
Silkworth, William D., 53, 63
Sinner's Prayer, 54. *See also* Oxford
    Group
sins, 90
Smith, Anne, 56
Smith, Randy. *See* Randy's story
Smith, Robert (Bob), 31, 57, 59,
    156–157
The Smithfield Café, 18
Snyder, Clarence, 32
sobriety, 126, 151–152
social Darwinism, 64
social instinct, 83
social intelligence, loss of, 122
social media, 118, 136
Social Security, 95
Social Security Disability Insurance
    (SSDI), 93, 95
societal sin
    defined, 91
    individual selfishness *vs.,*
        90–92
socio-economic dimension/factors,
    86, 143
soft skills, 124
soul pathologies, 128
Special Action Office of Drug
    Abuse Prevention, 85
spirit guides, 88
Spiritual Evolution (Vaillant), 65
spirituality, 181–183
    hardwired, 65–67
    James on, 54, 55, 56–59
    Jungian perspective, 60–63

moral psychology, 63–65
Oxford Group, 31–32, 54–56, 59
spiritual literature, 49
spiritual malady, 44
spiritual power, 44
SSDI. *See* Social Security Disability
    Insurance (SSDI)
SSRI. *See* selective serotonin
    reuptake inhibitor (SSRI)
staff-family communication, 144–145
staff/staffing, treatment center,
    142–143
Steele, Robert, 84–85
stimulant medications, 95–96, 123
stress and alienation, 81
Structure of Scientific Revolutions
    (Kuhn), xiv–xv
suboxone, 74
Suboxone, 145, 146
Substance Abuse and Mental Health
    Services Administration
    (SAMHSA), 130
Subsys, 102
success. *See also* treatment
    defining, 131–135
    indicators, 133–135
    innovation and activism, 135–136
    measuring, 132
Supplemental Security Income
    (SSI), 93
surrender, 45. *See also* prayer
Sweek, John. *See* John's story

tai chi, 144
textile industry, 84
Thatcher, Ebby, 53
Thornburgh, Dick, 108
Tick, Edward, 23, 127–128
TIRF REMS, 102
"tough-on-crime" legislation, 112

traditional cultures, 86–87
Transpersonal Psychology at
    Burlington College, 23, 28
trauma-informed approach, 144
treatment, 129–139
    access to, 148
    addicts receiving, percentage of,
        129–130
    effective program, 130–131
    successful, 131–135
treatment center, 141–149
    access to treatment, 148
    aftercare, 149
    clinical staff and team, 142–143
    community, 143–144
    family support, 144–145
    free services, 148–149
    MAT, 145–148
tribe, 138, 151–158. *See also*
    recovered addicts
    growing, 186
    members, 135–136
    mission, 153, 156–158
    recovered rather than
        recovering, 152
truth, 47
Tuke, William, 64
12 Traditions, 33–34
12-Step program, xvi–xviii, 31–52.
    See also recovered addicts;
    recovery
    as effective treatment modality, 37
    spirituality. *See* spirituality
    steps/constituents, 32–33, 44–52

underworld descent, 46
United States, xvi
    as addicted country, 36
    prison population, 105, 106
    private prisons, 110–111

unmanageability, 44
unselfishness, 55
U.S. Sentencing Commission, 106

Vaillant, George, 65–66, 67
Vancouver, xv
The Varieties of Religious Experience
     (James), 54, 55, 56–59
Vietnamese people, 127–128
Vietnam War, 75
vodka, 71

Waits, Tom, 72
The War of the Gods in Addiction
     (Schoen), 60
war on drugs, xv, 105–114. *See also*
     drug addicts
   terminology, 105
Warrior's Return (Tick), 127
Washington, D.C., 15

Webb, Gary, 73
welfare benefits, 73
Wesley, John, 51
Whitaker, Robert, 23, 173
White Bison, 49, 173
white knucklers, 40
Wilson, Bill, 31, 43, 48, 53, 63, 66–67,
     69, 90, 118, 153, 156–157, 176
withdrawal symptoms, xi, xii
World Series (1911), 71
World War I (WWI), 71
wounded healers, 51
Wright, Hamilton, 70
writing personal inventory, 45

yoga, 50, 144
YouTube, 155

Zimbardo, Philip, 122, 124
Zoja, Luigi, 126